WHO GOES THERE?

A CULTURAL HISTORY OF HEAVEN AND HELL

WHO GOES THERE?

REBECCA PRICE JANNEY

Moody Publishers

CHICAGO

All Scripture quotations, unless otherwise indicated, are taken from the *Holy Bible, New International Version*®. NIV®. Copyright © 1973, 1978, 1984 by International Bible Society. Used by permission of Zondervan Publishing House. All rights reserved.

Scripture quotations marked NLT are taken from the *Holy Bible, New Living Translation*, copyright © 1996. Used by permission of Tyndale House Publishers, Inc., Wheaton, Illinois 60189, U.S.A. All rights reserved.

All Web sites listed herein are accurate at the time of publication, but may change in the future or cease to exist. The listing of Web site references and resources does not imply publisher endorsement of the site's entire contents. Groups, corporations, and organizations are listed for informational purposes, and listing does not imply publisher endorsement of their activities.

Editor: Christopher Reese
Cover Design: Studio Gearbox
Cover Images: Photos.com, Veer, Getty Images
Interior Design: Smartt Guys design

Library of Congress Cataloging-in-Publication Data

Janney, Rebecca Price, 1957-
 Who goes there? : a cultural history of heaven and hell / Rebecca
Price Janney.
    p. cm.
 Includes bibliographical references.
 ISBN 978-0-8024-5493-5
 1. Future life. 2. Heaven. 3. Hell. 4. United States--Religion. I.
Title.
 BL535.J35 2009
 236'.20973--dc22
                 2008041177

This book is printed on acid free recycled paper containing 30% PCW (Post Consumer Waste) and manufactured in the United States of America by Bethany Press.

I dedicate this book to all the saints—those living and those who rest from their labors—who have enriched my life and pointed the way to heaven, especially my grandmothers, Pappy Harry, A. Ray Janney, and David R. Janney.

CONTENTS

1

WHAT ARE WE
THINKING?

Early in the morning of August 31, 1997, America awakened to
the stunning news that Princess Diana had died in a car accident in Paris. Five days later another woman whom millions
admired also died. Mother Teresa of Calcutta passed away at an
advanced age after a life of charitable works and faithfulness to God. In
the media there were many remarks about the significance of these two
women dying in the same week.

At the British embassy in Washington hordes of people created a
makeshift memorial of floral tributes, posters, stuffed animals, balloons,
and written messages. In the midst of it was a seven-foot-high plywood
placard on which someone had painted an angel with its arms out-
stretched. Across the top a message proclaimed, "The angels rejoice for
heaven welcomes Princess Diana and Mother Teresa."

While it is easy to understand how someone would believe that
Mother Teresa had gone to heaven, Princess Diana's case seemed less
certain. Most of her admirers simply assumed that she had gone there—
but why? Was it because of her beauty, fame, vulnerability, and tragic
death? Is that what it takes to go to heaven? Ten years later at a concert
in her honor, performer Diddy offered a musical homage in which he
encouraged the audience to raise their faces to the sky and tell Diana how
much they missed her, confident that she was "up there" listening.

Contemporary Americans tend to believe that all people go to heaven, and view the idea of hell as repugnant. There is a general assumption that unless someone was a child pornographer, racist, drug lord, or terrorist, he or she will go to heaven. (Of course, child pornographers, racists, drug lords, and terrorists think they will go to heaven, too.) Even then, Americans want to give people the benefit of the doubt, largely because they can't believe that a loving God would send people to such a place. If someone dies for a good cause, or as an innocent victim of a crime, it is taken for granted that they are destined for heaven. According to public opinion, this holds true for all of the victims of September 11, 2001.

It's not as if we come right out and say these things because most Americans haven't really thought them through. Our public statements, however, support this viewpoint. For example, after the attacks on America, a New York City firefighter told a reporter, "Heaven has some fire department now."[1] While he might have meant that many of the firefighters who died trying to save lives were worthy of heaven because of their religious faith, it is far more likely that he believed all of the rescuers automatically went to heaven based on the honorable way in which they had died. We can understand, of course, looking for hope and a bright side in the face of the tragic loss of life, especially on the scale of 9/11. Yet, most people haven't thought out the implications of these views logically, theologically, or otherwise. Rather, deep emotions have given rise to a common belief, and it seems unfeeling to question it. Such thinking is problematic.

In an ironic twist of this notion, Mohammed Atta, one of the 9/11 hijackers, also believed that as a result of that day's events, he would go to heaven. For a Muslim, martyrdom is the only sure way of getting to paradise. (In an unsettling way, this is close to the common American belief that if someone dies tragically or honorably, he or she is especially worthy of heaven.) Atta wrote these instructions to himself before his reprehensible act: "Be happy, optimistic, calm, because you are heading for a deed God loves and will accept. It will be the day, God willing, you spend with the women of paradise."[2]

On that September day Virginia DiChiara, who worked at the top of the North Tower for Cantor Fitzgerald, sustained third-degree burns over 30 percent of her body during her dramatic escape. Her recovery was as horrendous as the experience that prompted it. Of her a *Newsweek* reporter wrote, "She had gone to hell and then, slowly, painfully, come back."[3] Many others commented that people had experienced hell that day, but could they rationally support the belief that hell is something unspeakable that happens on earth rather than a place or condition in the afterlife?

A year and a half later when the space shuttle *Columbia* disintegrated upon reentry to earth, President George W. Bush told the stunned nation, "The same creator who names the stars also knows the names of the seven souls we lost today. The crew of the shuttle *Columbia* did not return safely to Earth, yet we can pray that all are safely home."[4] This was in sharp contrast to comments at the memorial service in Houston three days later by Captain Kent Rominger, chief of the astronaut corps. During the eulogy, he addressed the deceased heroes as if they could hear him. "I know you're listening. Please know you're in our hearts. We will always smile when we think of you."[5] So, because the astronauts were brave and noble and died tragically, they were in a conscious state, aware of all that was happening on earth. It's a warm and popular sentiment, but on what is this outlook based?

In a *Newsweek* end-of-the-year issue, writers paid tribute to celebrities who had died during the previous twelve months. Among them was ex-Beatle George Harrison, who had died of cancer in his fifties. The accolade read, "He was a cultural explorer, introducing Indian sitar to Western ears and adding Hindu thought to our consciousness. And he was a humanitarian, conceiving the all-star benefit with his 1971 Concert for Bangladesh. But let's face it, Harrison was a Beatle, first and forever. Not a bad deal for eternity."[6] Again, the assumption was that because he was good-hearted, innovative, and famous, Harrison attained eternal life. Nothing else about him mattered, not his personal morality or even his religious convictions.

When comedian Bob Hope died at the age of 100, a *Philadelphia In-quirer* cartoon by Tony Auth showed a joyous crowd of angels winging their way to an open door out of which laughter poured. Above it a sign read, "Now Appearing: Bob Hope," and to the side a smaller one said, "Unlimited Engagement."[7] Once more, there is the implicit belief that there is a heaven, and all well-meaning, well-loved people go there. To suggest otherwise is to be cruel and heartless.

Heaven isn't reserved only for the famous in modern American judgment. Anyone is qualified, especially if death came in a particularly poignant way. *Good Housekeeping* magazine featured a story about Ellen Kelly, a Rhode Island mother whose twenty-year-old daughter, Brigid, was tragically killed by a drunk driver. In it, the article mentions a ritual that Kelly observes at the place where she had scattered her daughter's ashes and in which she finds a degree of solace. "Ellen goes to Goose-berry Beach to talk with her daughter. 'I tell her what I've done during my day, what Elise (her other daughter) has done. I mention people I've talked to,' she says. 'I tell Brigid I miss her, and every time I leave, I tell her to have a good night and that I love her. I say, 'I'll see you tomorrow.' And then I cry.'"[8]

All of these stories represent the current American view of the af-terlife. For how long have we been thinking in this way? How did past generations view heaven and hell, and how did that affect the way they lived? Death and what comes next are crucial aspects of life, and we take a huge risk if we cannot support what we believe, especially if exclusive religious claims are true.

One of the world's most identifiable and popular works of art is Au-guste Rodin's *The Thinker*. Created in 1881, this brilliant sculpture has come to represent man's search for knowledge. On the set of the annual college tournaments of *Jeopardy!* it symbolizes intellectual pursuit. *The Thinker* is, however, far more than that. Rodin created it in conjunc-tion with his work *The Gates of Hell*, inspired by Dante's epic poem, *The*

Divine Comedy. The Thinker was a naked man contemplating a troubling scene—the punishment of souls writhing in hell because they turned their backs on God. Particularly disturbing are its images of children in torment, those whom we think of as innocence personified.

Rodin lived in the modern era when scientific thought prompted people to pursue and find universal truth about life and death. For secularists that truth would be based on scientific inquiry; for religionists, on reason and a rational, intellectual study of their holy books. When a person arrived at that attainable truth, he or she could rest assured of their convictions. This is not so in our postmodern society where all truth is seen as relative and not universal, as specific only to individuals and their environments. It is ironic that with all of our personally held convictions we are arriving at the same conclusion: All good people go to a good place, usually called heaven, where they look down on us, and that there is no hell except for the worst of the worst human beings—and maybe not even then.

When Tim Russert died in 2008, he left behind two heartwarming books about fathers. In *Wisdom of Our Fathers*, he recounted the story of Diane Cole Mathis, who shared a special love for the New York Yankees with her father. Although he died when Diane was only twelve, she says she still feels that he is with her, and she looks forward to their heavenly reunion. "Whenever I see anything with a Yankees logo, something pulls at my heart. It could be my dad, telling me that when we meet again I should bring his chair and, if I can find one, an ice-cold bottle of Ballantine beer."[9] Such sentiments make hurting people feel better, but they are very much like drinking alcohol in a snowstorm. While it makes a freezing person feel warm, it is dangerous because it's a false warmth. People have been known to freeze to death feeling warm. Jesus alone can provide the comfort and assurance that we all crave.

LET'S START AT THE VERY BEGINNING

When singer Johnny Cash died, many Americans met the news of his death with sadness that a beloved star was gone. That he was seventy-one, his wife had passed away just a few months earlier, and the Man in Black had been suffering physically, however, removed some of the sting. It came as no shock that he died. The same could not be said, however, about actor John Ritter's death a day earlier. No one expected the effervescent fifty-four-year-old to fall ill suddenly on his sitcom set and die of a torn aorta.

That evening on *Entertainment Tonight*, a reporter took her camera crew to actor Henry Winkler's home, and she greeted him with a tearful embrace. She was the last entertainment correspondent to have interviewed Ritter, and Winkler, one of the deceased actor's best friends, had been making an appearance on Ritter's show when the actor became ill. Winkler was understandably broken up as he told the story. At one point the reporter looked Winkler in the eye and said, "*I know* John is up there looking down on you and that he would just like to wrap his arms around you and tell you to keep on going." Winkler looked as if he wanted to believe this but wasn't so sure. He began his response with, "If he is up there . . ."

That reporter's statement of faith would irritate most seminary professors who carefully examine the Bible's original texts to discern their meaning, parsing Greek and deciphering Hebrew for accuracy. On what was *her* sure and certain belief based, her bold "I know," followed by her assurance that the comedian was "up there" and at that moment "looking down" on Henry Winkler—not his wife, not his kids, but Henry Winkler? She also professed to know exactly how he would respond to his friend's distress.

One of the most prevalent contemporary-America beliefs about life after death is the concept that the dead are "up there looking down" on friends and loved ones. During the final ceremonies on the last day of a Phillies game at Philadelphia's Veterans Stadium, broadcaster Harry Kalas paid homage to his late colleague Rich "Whitey" Ashburn while the TV camera showed a fan holding a sign reading, "Whitey is with us, Harry." Other announcers said they also were sure Ashburn was there. Where does this idea come from? Is it trustworthy? This book will examine what others long ago believed and what they have passed down to contemporary Americans. Because the United States is a "melting pot" of cultures and religious beliefs, it is important to analyze what some of those major groups have believed historically about heaven and hell.

∽o∽

If *Entertainment Tonight* had existed centuries ago in India, and the reporter mentioned earlier recorded the reaction of a man whose best friend had died unexpectedly, it might have gone something like this:

"Please know how sorry I am to hear that Abhi has died," the newswoman might have said. "I know how close you were to him."

"Yes, yes, it was quite a shock."

"You were with him not long before, is that not true?"

"Indeed I was. He had not been feeling well, but we had no idea that his sickness would result in death."

As the friend began to weep, the reporter tried to comfort him. Drawing closer she said, "Abhi was a good man. He worked hard, provided well for his family, was generous to friends and strangers alike, and he kept a moral life. I am sure that his karma will be favorable and that he will return in a higher form of life the next time."

That conversation provides an abbreviated look at what ancient Indians believed when Hinduism began to develop. The most important of that religion's texts is the *Bhagavad Gita*, and in it there is a story about Krishna, the incarnated god of creation, coming to a Prince Arjuna. Krishna informs the royal son that the soul's life does not end at death and, therefore, the life of the body itself is of no great significance. What really matters is the way a person lives, whether or not he fulfills his special place in society. Those actions produce consequences or *karma*. When a person dies, he enters a protracted cycle of death and rebirth. If his karma is favorable, his next life will be positive, resulting in a higher state of integrity and peace. If not, he will return in a form—even as an insect or animal—that enables him to learn, grow, and fulfill his purpose for that life. Apparently, fictitious Abhi had lived in such a good way that his friends believed the outlook for his next life was favorable.

∞○∞

Death was a crucial theme for the ancient Egyptians, who spent a great deal of time and money preparing for what came next. They had a cult around the idea of the afterlife, along with highly structured ceremonies. The common belief was that life did go on, that people continued as themselves, with needs that had to be met in death just as in life, such as for food and clothing. It was up to the living to ensure that their loved ones met those requirements; otherwise, the dead might justifiably haunt them. The concepts of order and balance in society were fundamental to Egyptians, and caring for the needs of the dead was part of what kept the social order from falling into chaos. It was serious business to neglect one's obligations to the deceased.

Egyptians had a positive sense about what the afterlife would be like, but they also believed that in order for a person to enjoy it, his good deeds would have to outweigh the bad. Their overall optimism led to a belief that most people would enjoy a happy afterlife. When a person died, along with material goods, messages would also be buried with him as evidence of his character. Osiris, the Egyptian god of the Nile, was believed to oversee the journey from death to the beyond, which included a time of judgement for the individual.

∽o∾

Others living in the ancient Middle East developed far less sanguine ideas about the afterlife than the Egyptians. In Persia, for example, a philosopher developed a system called Zoroastrianism in which equal powers of good and evil battled it out for supremacy in the world. Everyone's actions were recorded in a book of life, and when a person died he went to heaven for a reading of the accounts and words of his life. If his good deeds outweighed the bad, he would head to paradise. If the opposite were true, eternal suffering would result in a hellish place. In case there was an equal balance between the good and the bad, the person would enter a state of limbo until a last judgment of mankind by the gods and a final decision on each person's ultimate fate.[1]

While the Hebrews also had a strong sense of good and evil, they did not view them as equal entities like Zoroastrians. There was only one God, Yahweh, unequalled in power. Although Satan was the prince of darkness, he was clearly not regarded as a deity. Early on, Jews had a concept of an afterlife, but it wasn't completely developed, nor was it especially comforting. According to Eugene Merrill, "The New Testament concept of heaven and hell is lacking here [i.e., in the OT] and, in fact, is nowhere to be found in the Old Testament."[2] All dead people were understood to go to a place under the earth known as *sheol* or simply "the grave." R. Laird Harris describes it as "a poorly defined region from which there was no resurrection, and in which there was no reward or punishment."[3] Harris observes that if *sheol* really does mean simply "the grave" in certain Old Testament passages, it "gives us a picture of a typical Palestinian tomb, dark, dusty, with mingled bones and where 'this poor lisping stammering tongue lies silent in the grave.' All the souls of men do not go to one place. But all people go to the grave."[4] However, believers in Yahweh were hopeful about their ultimate destiny. According to Harris, "The future life is affirmed in many places in the Old Testament, although details are not given. The intermediate state and the destiny of the wicked get less emphasis."[5]

∞○∞

Most Americans think of Confucianism as China's major religion, but it actually is more of an ethical system to help society function smoothly and orderly. According to Confucius (c. 551– c. 479 BC), it is much more important to be concerned with this world than with anything supernatural or metaphysical. For him, the highest good was to achieve harmony between oneself and society. Morality was what kept people wanting to do right and to be in accord with others. He believed conforming to the societal good was enough to occupy a person's energies without dwelling on an afterlife. In China, however, people often prayed to their ancestors for help. While Confucius did not authorize this, he believed that ancestors provided a special continuity between the generations and so should be revered, if not worshiped.[6]

Along came Lao-tze, another Chinese philosopher at the time of Confucius, whose teachings merged with old folk beliefs and who emphasized the supernatural. He tended toward a reincarnational view of the afterlife in which people took on forms that were appropriate to the kind of life they had led. Perfection, he said, could be attained in one of those life cycles, but was a rare occurrence.[7]

∞○∞

For the ancient Greeks, from which so much Western thought originated, life after death inspired keen debates between their best philosophers, including Plato and Homer. Overall, however, there was "no clear theory about the afterlife . . . and no substantial hopes were based upon them."[8] According to Homer, "A kind of wraith of the dead man vanished to the underworld," which was an unhappy place, one of shadows, "joyless, eventless, meaningless."[9] There was a state of bliss, as well as one of punishment, but the former could only be experienced by a "few select heroes."[10]

Plato believed that the soul preexisted the body and was independent of it, while Aristotle didn't have much time for anything mystical. If *Entertainment Tonight* had interviewed him after a friend's death, he would have derided the reporter's obsession about what happened next. For Aristotle, the main thing would be what his friend had done and been in life and whether it had brought him satisfaction or grief. He did believe that people have some sort of divine "spark" in them, and that would go on, but not in any personal way.[11] Democritus was even more blunt, writing, "Death ends all, but is no evil, since in it there is no consciousness remaining."[12]

Not all Greeks were satisfied to relegate their emotions to sheer logic, though, and some of them turned to various "mystery religions" that promised a better deal in an afterlife. The most significant of these cults emerged near Athens around the goddesses Persephone and Demeter. But for the majority of Greeks, what happened at death remained uncertain.[13]

∞◦∞

The ancient Romans emphasized life in this world as opposed to speculating about what might come after death, but that did not satisfy the ache of their hearts at the graves of their loved ones, or give them peace about their own end. What the intelligentsia promoted, when they spoke in terms of the afterlife at all, included a borrowing of philosophical and religious concepts from the Greeks. For example, the Greek Epicureans totally denied that anything came after death, and they had Roman followers who went by the slogan, "Eat, drink, and be merry, for tomorrow we die." On the other hand there were Romans who followed the Greek Stoics who said that there are no rewards or punishments in death, rather, that virtue in this life is its own reward, and vice results in its own punishment. They asserted that there was a soul but held out little hope for its survival.[14] None of this was particularly helpful to the masses. One Greek philosopher often mentioned by educated Romans was Socrates, and he promoted the idea that there was "either a happy afterlife or painless nothingness," which must have left his listeners scratching their heads.[15]

The Roman orator Cicero believed that anything existing of the divine in human beings was immortal and that, according to an old Roman tradition, there was a "remote region among the stars," a happy place for good people to go when they died. For him, there was no place of punishment, which he dismissed as the product of an old wives' tale.[16] Virgil believed that most souls went to an underworld, and bad people suffered the "punishments of Tartarus," a place in Hades—the underground of the dead—reserved for the worst kind of offenders.[17]

Most people in the Roman Empire who felt spiritually inclined turned toward Oriental religions such as Cybele, or Worship of the Great Mother, which involved sexually depraved rites. They also followed Asia Minor's Attis, Persia's Mithras, as well as Isis and Serapis from Egypt, each of which emphasized regeneration and an afterlife. In all of these, the soul was said to experience rebirth. A redeemer-god and various mythologies usually involving a dying and rising god were also part of those beliefs.[18] When Christianity penetrated Rome, a majority of the empire's citizens were preoccupied by, but uncertain about, life after death.

∾o∾

In pre-Columbian America, afterlife beliefs took on a far different tone. The Mayans believed in layers of heaven, thirteen to be exact, while nine worlds existed below the earth. At death, people merged with the gods, becoming one, and their descendents then worshiped them. Similarly, the Aztecs thought there were heavenly layers above the earth and that those who died as warriors in battle, merchants on distant trips who passed away, and women who died in childbirth, got to go to those heavens where they became the sun's companions. Everyone else endured the nine worlds below, including a hellish region with nine rivers called Mictlan, which dead souls took four years to cross. Then they would simply vanish. The Incas believed that two souls resided in people, one of them remained with the body at death, and the other returned to its place of origin.[19]

Most native North Americans also believed in the immortality of the soul, asserting that the afterlife would be full of all that made this life secure and pleasant.[20] The Iroquois of the Northeast thought the dead became ghosts who went to an afterlife that became interwoven with the life of the person's tribe. Winter festivals were conducted for the benefit of those ghosts, who were believed to take part unseen in the dancing and games. During raiding parties, the ghosts would also be present, but they would not participate. Contrary to popular opinion, Native Americans did not believe in a "happy hunting ground" because this clashed with their conviction that ghosts did not eat food.[21]

Death brought about a complex ritual that included fasting, wakefulness, a ban on speaking the dead person's name, and blowing ashes on the corpse to appease the person's spirit. If assuaged, it would return after three days to drink water from a pot laid at the corpse's head. Should rippling water be present in the pot, this was a sign that the deceased would not trouble the living.[22]

∽०∾

Our ancient ancestors speculated, marveled about, and feared the afterlife—what it was, where it was, and if indeed it was. Twenty-first-century Americans have the blessings and drawbacks of centuries of meticulously constructed beliefs from every possible culture and every conceivable angle of understanding. Each American is the product of at least one of those religions or philosophies, often more than one. What has happened to us is similar at least in one way to the ancient

Romans who built upon the foundations of their own earliest traditions and folklore, then integrated the teachings of the Greek and Oriental philosophies.

At the time of Christianity's advent into their culture, most Romans, like the majority of Americans today, were theistic, although they hadn't really settled on one way of thinking about God or gods. They also felt concerned about life after death, wanting to believe it was real and true, fearing that it might not be, and wondering where truth really lay. Like modern Americans, those Romans had mostly abandoned the traditions of their ancestors. They adopted other cultures' views, creating a syncretism that left many in doubt about life after death. Scholars were generally contemptuous of or confused about the whole idea, while the majority of Romans—although they may not have known why—clung to popular concepts. L. P. Wilkinson summed up the state of Roman belief, but he could have been referring to America today:

> The nature and extent of belief in survival is hard to assess.... "Farewell forever" continues to be the sentiment of many tombs; "I was, I am not, I care not." But the great majority ostensibly attest belief.... What cannot be assessed is how much was pure convention, how much hope that went beyond mere sentiment.[23]

AMERICAN
ORIGINS

D uring his lifetime George Whitefield traveled the thirteen original colonies, preaching over eighteen thousand sermons.[1] On Whitefield's death-bed, an attending minister took note of his colleague that "he felt the pleasures of heaven in his raptured soul, which made his countenance shine like the unclouded sun."[2] After delivering his last sermon the night before, Whitefield had exclaimed:

> I go! I go to rest prepared. My sun has arisen and by the aid of heaven has given light to many. It is now about to set. . . . No! It is about to rise to the zenith of immortal glory . . . O thought divine! I shall soon be in a world where time, age, pain and sorrow are unknown. My body fails, my spirit expands. How willingly I would ever live to preach Christ! But I die to be with Him![3]

This was the majority opinion in colonial times. In fact, when the Revolutionary War broke out in 1775, 99.8 percent of Americans claimed to be Christians, and of those, 98.4 percent were Protestants.[4] America was at the beginning a gathering of people from Europe, Christian in practice or background, dominated by English Protestants, and sprinkled with Spanish and French Roman Catholic colonies in Florida, "Louisiana," and parts of the West and Southwest. According to Dr. Peter Lillback, the colonists were tutored on the historic confessions of the Christian faith with the Protestant perspective dominating. On the way to America in the spring of 1630, Puritan John Winthrop preached about this new land becoming a city on a hill for all the world to see. His desire and that of his people wasn't conformity to a certain style of Christianity, but to be such an example to the world that those outside the faith would desire to know its God, live productively, and gain an eternal reward. According to Lillback, those people had "absolutely nothing much to grab on to here. They lived in a pre-medical, pre-modern world, and they had nothing—a wilderness to walk into, an exploration of the unknown. Death was very real. It may come at any moment. They lived on the edge of life."[5]

The old Granary Cemetery in Boston that dates back to the mid-1660s bears witness to Lillback's assertion. On one gravestone, three children are commemorated, one who died at three days, another at two weeks, the last at eighteen months. Another reads, "In Memory of Alexander MacKay Jun, Son of Capt Alexr & Mrs Ruthey Mackay, Who died Nov 29th 1787, in the 16th year, of his Age." Mary "Mother" Goose is buried there also, having died at forty-two. Also on her gravestone is inscribed the death of her fifteen-month-old child. Many of those buried at Granary died in their twenties and thirties. Several markers portray a grim-looking skull and crossbones, reminders of the proximity to death in which those people lived.

Today, many argue that those who came to America were far more interested in economic gain than heavenly glory. However, even those who settled the Jamestown colony, which was largely a business venture, possessed strong Christian beliefs, and they desired both religious liberty and the opportunity to share their faith with the native inhabitants. According to the 1606 Virginia Charter, the latter was one of the main purposes for coming to America. When the colonists landed at Cape Henry, one of the first things they did was to set up a wooden cross. One story in particular demonstrates the aspiration of some within the Jamestown settlement to evangelize the Native Americans, rather than simply to make a lot of money.[6]

಄ംഔ

After their arrival, the English received a frequent visitor to their fort, an Indian princess whose father ruled a few dozen Tidewater tribes. When their supplies ran low, Pocahontas could be counted upon to bring food to ease their hunger. Captain Samuel Argall detained the adolescent in the spring of 1613 as a pawn to secure the release of several English prisoners held by Tidewater Indians. Pocahontas received good treatment, and her father even cooperated with the captain's plan. During that time, a widower named John Rolfe taught her about his God and, concerned for her eternal soul, urged her to become a believer in Jesus Christ. She received Christian baptism and took the name Rebecca. The following April she married Rolfe.

The foundation of American beliefs about salvation, heaven, and hell was laid by European Christians like Rolfe and Winthrop. Alexis de Tocqueville, who visited the country in the early nineteenth century, observed that Americans "combine the notions of Christianity and liberty so intimately that it is impossible to make them conceive of one without the other."[7] In those earliest years, Protestantism was the form of Christianity that dominated American life. The official beginning of that religious movement came on October 31, 1517, when the German monk Martin Luther took his church to task on several points of faith. While there had been other expressions of protest against church corruption and calls for a return to a purer form of Christianity, Luther was "the first outstanding leader" of Protestantism.[8] His major problem with the Roman Catholic Church centered around issues of heaven and hell.

಄ംഔ

Luther was born in 1483 and raised in the traditions of medieval Roman Catholicism. According to one scholar, "The young Martin grew up to fear God, to believe in the reality of heaven, hell, angels, saints, the Devil, and demons. He stood in terror of Christ as judge, but he also

believed in the efficacy of the intercession of the Virgin Mary, the apostles, and the saints."[9] One day while Luther was studying law in 1505, a
lightning bolt nearly struck him, bringing about a seminal change in his
life. He was so terrified of hell that Luther pledged himself to become
a monk, thinking that would pacify God's anger and lead to salvation.
Choosing a rigorous order, the young man "mortified his body. He fast-
ed, sometimes for days on end and without a morsel of food. He gave
himself to prayers and vigils beyond those required by the rule of his order. He went to confession, often daily and for hours at a time."[10]

All of his intensity and service to God left him exhausted spiritually.
Then one day he had a revelation prompted by Romans 1:17: "The righteous shall live by faith." It dawned on him that good works do not earn
God's favor or get someone to heaven. Rather, they are products of a
faith in God that alone wins His grace and secures salvation. That is why
Luther became especially disturbed by a certain practice in the Roman
Catholic Church. Arising in the Middle Ages, *indulgences* were a way in
which the faithful could get the pope to secure forgiveness for their sins,
or the sins of others. It didn't matter whether those sins were past, present, or future, or the other person being prayed for was dead. All this
could be had for a price that had enriched pontiffs and their supporters.
One Dominican monk "hawked" indulgences with the zeal of a medieval
infomercial, claiming that as soon as the money fell into the coffers, a
soul was released from purgatory (in Roman Catholic theology, a provi-
sional place for the dead to be cleansed before entering heaven).

Luther was not pleased, especially considering his prior spiritual suffering over the state of his soul and the great revelation that had set him
free. On October 31, 1517, he posted a list of 95 theses on the door of the
castle church at Wittenberg, a kind of university bulletin board in which
academics invited debate about all sorts of subjects. Such postings were
not uncommon; what resulted from this one, however, turned European
Christianity upside down. Luther maintained that no pope had power
to free anyone from purgatory and that claiming to do so gave people a

false sense of security about eternity, as well as the wrong theology about heaven and hell.

Aided by the printing press, various movements within the "Reformation" spread throughout Europe. The key component in them all was the concept of justification by faith in Jesus Christ alone. Those refusing belief in Christ or trying to attain salvation in some other way were hell-bound by their own choice.

∽o∾

Another major Reformation figure, second only to Luther, was the French-born (1509) theology and law student, John Calvin. He converted to Christianity suddenly in his early twenties, then went to Basel, which became a strong Protestant center. At twenty-six, he wrote the seminal book of the Reformation, *The Institutes of the Christian Religion*, setting forth "the entire cosmic drama of creation, sin, and redemption under the sovereign will of God."[11] The hinge of his teaching was the doctrine of *predestination*—that God has chosen some people to be saved (go to heaven) and some to be damned (go to hell). He believed that people should accept God's choice and His justice, rather than argue about whether or not this was fair, thus putting themselves in the foolish position of setting up a "standard of human justice as the standard by which to measure the justice of God."[12]

During the sixteenth century, Europe experienced many religious wars as political forces aligned with Protestantism and Roman Catholicism battled for control of the continent and Great Britain. In the latter country, King Henry VIII created the Anglican Church (Church of England) early in the 1530s when he broke with Rome for more personal and political than purely spiritual purposes. It didn't take many decades before that particular church needed to be reformed itself and dissenters appeared. The Puritans were one group deeply dissatisfied by the church's clergymen, especially their fondness for ornate vestments and pompous liturgical practices. By contrast, they stressed stark simplicity in worship and clerical garb, the importance of Bible study, intellectual development, and a strong work ethic. They also upheld the hallmark of the Protestant Reformation, *sola fide*, the conviction that faith in Jesus Christ was the only way to heaven, not good works of any amount or nature. Influenced by Calvin, the Puritans maintained that God had determined in advance who would go to heaven and who would not. Their beliefs and practices became "a social force [that] has been [a] pervasive and permanent influence in the United States, extending far beyond New England and the colonial period."[13]

In the late sixteenth century, two groups formed out of the Puritan movement, those who considered it possible to reform the Anglican Church, and the Separatists or Pilgrims, who thought it best to leave and "let the dead bury their dead." In 1609 the Pilgrims left England for Holland, where they lived untroubled by the authorities for ten years. Nevertheless, these were a people on a mission, and they began to grow restless. They didn't want only to live unmolested by the law; they wanted to make a mark on the world in the name of God. Passages from the Old Testament, in particular the experiences of ancient Israel, provided the backdrop and motivation for the Pilgrims' decision to sail to America on the *Mayflower* in 1620. By 1628 many Puritans were ready to follow their Pilgrim counterparts to New England in search of religious freedom. They were able to secure a royal charter to establish what they called the Massachusetts Bay Colony led by a governor, lawyer John Winthrop. In the early spring of 1630, Winthrop, one of his sons, and over eight hundred other people headed for New England on sixteen ships. Halfway across the Atlantic, Winthrop preached a sermon that set the tone for the endeavor. Standing on the deck of the *Arbella*, he proclaimed a grand vision:

> We must Consider that we shall be as a City upon a Hill, the eyes of all people are upon us; so that if we shall deal falsely with our God in this work we have undertaken and so cause him to withdraw his present help from us, we shall open the mouths of enemies to speak evil of the ways of

God and all professours for Gods [sic] sake.[14]

Not only were the Puritans going to heaven—they planned to take the entire New World with them.

FANNING THE
FLAMES

A ccording to a popular bumper sticker, "Life is short—then you die." Never was that truer than in colonial America when the average life span was just fifty-six years. Many people died far younger.[1] Death came from complications in childbirth, from infectious diseases, poor sanitation, and lack of medical knowledge. This was "a society radically different from our own, in which frail and fleeting human life was lived out in the expectation of salvation or damnation, eternal happiness or torment."[2] Daniel A. Cohen refers to it as "a culture preoccupied with the proximity of death."[3]

When a measles epidemic broke out in 1713 in Boston, the Rev. Cotton Mather observed that it was going to be a time of trouble for all of the families living there. He saw it as his job to prepare them to meet their Maker. He was a man of sorrows himself; he outlived two of three wives and twelve of his fifteen children. During the measles outbreak, he buried a wife and three children, including newborn twins. Although Mather was grief-stricken, he said it comforted him that God had "extinguished in [my wife] the fear of death." Likewise, before his two-year-old daughter died, she told her father she was confident she was going to be with Jesus. Crushed in spirit, he resolved to continue ministering to the people of Boston, showing them "a patient submission to the will of God."[4]

Colonial Americans faced death with a measured acceptance, believing that it was part of a fallen world, and that it was a person's responsibility to accept the bad with the good. The anger that people so often express toward God today after a loved one dies wasn't part of the early American spirit. The colonists saw themselves as sinners who deserved nothing but condemnation from God, who in His love gave them grace instead. If anyone was to be on the defensive, it was them.

In spite of the Christian foundation of early America, in the opening decades of the eighteenth century, enthusiasm about spreading the gospel throughout the New World had become smoke and embers in many communities. During that time, a new wave of divine activity broke out, what Peter Marshall calls "a reawakening of a deep national desire for the Covenant Way of life. This yearning," he says, "did not die with the passing of the Puritan era, but only went dormant. It was a desire which would produce a new generation of clergymen who would help to prepare America to fight for her life."[5]

Among that group was one of the Great Awakening's key figures, George Whitefield, who observed at the beginning of the revival, "The generality of preachers talk of an unknown and unfelt Christ. The reason why congregations have been so dead is because they had dead men preaching to them. How can dead men beget living children?"[6] One minister who had been laboring for nearly ten years with less than dramatic results was Jonathan Edwards, a son of the New England elite who entered Yale at fourteen. Influenced by the liberal ideals of the Enlightenment, especially that reason is the source of all authority, Edwards nevertheless planned to become a pastor. He accepted his first charge at seventeen, but just before going to New York to begin the position, he experienced a profound conversion to Christ. Six years later he moved to Northampton, Massachusetts, one of New England's earliest settled towns, to minister there with his maternal grandfather. He discovered early on that the descendants of the zealous Puritans and Pilgrims had exchanged their spiritual heritage for a love of ease.

Although he preached deeply and thoughtfully about the individual's need for salvation, Edwards had a dry, monotonous style, and he avoided making eye contact with his congregation. When he began a sermon series about justification by faith alone, he began to notice startling changes in his parishioners, including a greater seriousness about their spiritual state. One woman, who was notorious for her "company keeping," came to Christ, and soon many others followed. Edwards wrote in his account of the revival that followed, "This seems to have been a very extraordinary dispensation of Providence: God has, in many respects, gone out of, and much beyond his usual and ordinary way."[7] He noted that the revival touched people of all ages and socioeconomic conditions, and that a hallmark of the movement was a "great and earnest concern about the great things of religion and the eternal world . . . all other talk but about spiritual and eternal things was soon thrown by."[8]

Church historian Martin Marty says, "Jonathan Edwards and his colleagues preached for decision, conversion, the regeneration of men. The potentially faithful were told that their decisions were fateful for their personal destinies and for the shape of community."[9] A major characteristic of the revival was that as the people became convicted about their need for Christ to attain eternal life, their present lives changed radically. Edwards wrote of the "glorious alteration" that occurred when God poured out His Spirit upon Northampton. He wrote, "In the spring and summer following, anno 1735, the town seemed to be full of the presence of God: it never was so full of love, nor so full of joy, and yet so full of distress as it was then."[10] Whereas before the revival about thirty people a year came to Christ, that many and more were making professions of faith each week. Most of them, Edwards discovered, were "awakened with a sense of their miserable condition" before a holy and just God and "the danger they are in of perishing eternally."[11]

No one was better at describing the fearful torments of hell than Edwards, whose sermon, "Sinners in the Hands of an Angry God," is one of the best known in American history. In it he said of the unregenerate sinner:

The God that holds you over the pit of hell, much as one holds a spider, or some loathsome insect over the fire, abhors you, and is dreadfully provoked: his wrath towards you burns like fire; he looks upon you as worthy of nothing else, but to be cast into the fire; he is of purer eyes than to bear to have you in his sight; you are ten thousand times more abominable in his eyes, than the most hateful venomous serpent is in ours. You have offended him infinitely more than ever a stubborn rebel did his prince; and yet it is nothing but his hand that holds you from falling into the fire every moment. It is to be ascribed to nothing else, that you did not go to hell the last night; that you was suffered to awake again in this world, after you closed your eyes to sleep. And there is no other reason to be given, why you have not dropped into hell since you arose in the morning, but that God's hand has held you up. There is no other reason to be given why you have not gone to hell, since you have sat here in the house of God, provoking his pure eyes by your sinful wicked manner of attending his solemn worship. Yea, there is nothing else that is to be given as a reason why you do not this very moment drop down into hell.

Furthermore, the sinner would be wise to meditate upon what hell would be like:

O sinner! Consider the fearful danger you are in: it is a great furnace of wrath, a wide and bottomless pit, full of the fire of wrath, that you are held over in the hand of that God, whose wrath is provoked and incensed as much against you, as against many of the damned in hell. You hang by a slender thread, with the flames of divine wrath flashing about it, and ready every moment to singe it, and burn it asunder; and you have no interest in any Mediator, and nothing to lay hold of to save yourself, nothing to keep off the flames of wrath, nothing of your own, nothing that you ever have done, nothing that you can do, to induce God to spare you one moment.[12]

F. L. Chapell says that when Edwards delivered that message, "such was the influence upon the congregation, which had assembled in a careless mood, that some of them actually caught hold of the benches to save themselves from slipping into hell."[13]

Edwards was also much interested in heaven, and his view of it was according to a traditional, theocentric model. "By the middle of the seventeenth century the notion of the theocentric heaven had spread throughout western Christianity," according to Colleen McDannell and Bernhard Lang. People believed that "heaven is for God, and the eternal life of the saints revolves around a divine center. . . . Heaven is fundamentally a religious place—a center of worship, of divine revelation, and pious conversations with sacred characters."[14] Eternity would be spent contemplating and worshiping the God of all creation, and in so doing, humanity would find complete fulfillment and joy.

❧

The revival that cleaned up Northampton spread to the other colonies as well. In New Jersey the Dutch Reformed pastor Theodore Frelinghuysen had been preaching about heartfelt conversion since his arrival in America in 1720, appalled by the spiritual apathy he found among the colonists there. He went on to influence William Tennent who, with his son Gilbert, preached salvation by faith in Pennsylvania. In addition, the Presbyterian Samuel Davies labored toward that end in Virginia while David Brainerd ministered among the Native Americans. According to Peter Marshall and David Manuel, "Brainerd was in open awe of the power of God which fell on one village after another as he preached. Indians would change so dramatically that skeptical whites would come to the meetings to mock, only to be converted themselves!"[15] What Brainerd described as an "irresistible force of a mighty torrent or swelling deluge" brought many to salvation and the promise of a glorious hereafter.[16]

These "evangelical" preachers came to be known as "New Lights," and the old guard ministers who had been presiding over spiritually dead congregations ridiculed their unconventional ways. They asked what business William Tennent had training farm boys to preach the gospel and referred contemptuously to Tennent's training school as "the log college" (it provided the foundation for Princeton University). On

the other hand, Gilbert Tennent preached against "the danger of an unconverted ministry." He told his people, "As a faithful ministry is a great
ornament, blessing, and comfort to the church of God (even the feet of
such messengers are beautiful), so, on the contrary, an ungodly ministry
is a great curse and judgment. These caterpillars labor to devour every
green thing."[17]

While God's Spirit provoked strong passions that long lay dormant
in Colonial America, He also was raising up a prophet across the sea in
England to further the Great Awakening. George Whitefield preached
with such zeal that more traditional clergy refused to allow him in their
pulpits, both in his native England and in the colonies. Like Edwards,
Whitefield seemed an unlikely choice for such a position considering
that he had play-acted through school rather than studied, and finally
dropped out at age fifteen to help run the family business. Unlike Edwards, Whitefield dazzled audiences when he spoke. During his years
at Oxford University's Pembroke College, he became friends with two
brothers, Charles and John Wesley, earnest young men who sought a
deeper experience of God than was usually offered by the ordained clergy
of that day. Although young Whitefield strove on a level similar to Martin
Luther's to feel right with God, a sense of spiritual peace about his eternal state eluded him. The breakthrough came when he read an obscure
book, *The Life of God in the Soul of Man*, by the Scotsman Henry Scou-
gal, who encouraged people to cease striving and allow the Spirit of God
to dwell within them. Thoroughly excited by this discovery, Whitefield
set out to tell his fellow Englishmen that salvation was God's gift, not
something they could earn by good works.

That proved to be a difficult task in a country where people attended
church out of a social obligation and the pastors' sermons were as dry
as the dust that Whitefield had cleaned out of his family's inn as a youth.
He desired to preach in a fresh, new way, and he called upon his flair
for drama to call people to salvation. It mortified staid Englishmen
that Whitefield often shouted and danced, and sometimes cried while

speaking of people living hopelessly apart from Christ.[18] Fellow pastors told Whitefield that when he came to their churches, he was to "tone it down," stop prancing and flailing, or not be so loud, but he simply couldn't comply. The hope that Christ offered to lost people for this life and the one to come kept him moving.

In 1739 Whitefield felt compelled by God to go to America because he'd heard that the churches there were as dead as England's. The Americans weren't sure what to make of him at first with his theatrical ways, although the clergy tended to write him off as an "enthusiast." He used his powerful voice and gesturing to speak boldly about sin and salvation, heaven and hell, as he called people to exchange their head knowledge of Christ for a heartfelt personal commitment. The common people loved him. Samuel Eliot Morison observed that, "his messages were simple, direct, and taught the basic doctrines of being born again or being justified by faith. But to people who had not heard this clearly explained before, it was like a lightning shock to the heart."[19] Whitefield preached up and down the Eastern seaboard, drawing the size of crowds that contemporary rock stars entertain. When he took his message to Philadelphia, Whitefield drew the curiosity of a young printer named Benjamin Franklin who observed:

> The multitudes of all sects and denominations that attended his sermons were enormous, and it was a matter of speculation to me, who was one of the number, to observe the extraordinary influence of his oratory upon his hearers, and how much they admired and respected him notwithstanding his common abuse of them by assuring them that they were naturally half beasts and half devils.[20]

"It was wonderful," Franklin said, "to see the change soon made in the manners of our inhabitants. From being thoughtless or indifferent about religion, it seemed as if all the world were growing religious, so that one could not walk through the town in an evening without hearing psalms sung in different families of every street."[21] Like most Philadelphians, Franklin was enthralled by the itinerant preacher, but he went largely to hear how far Whitefield's voice could project, not to improve his spiritual condition. He'd heard stories that Whitefield had spoken to as many as twenty-five thousand people at a time, but he was skeptical, and so in true Ben Franklin style he conducted an experiment. While Whitefield spoke, Franklin seemed immune to the stirring message about sin and salvation, heaven and hell, as he calculated that the Englishman could indeed be heard by more than thirty thousand people.

Whitefield and Franklin became the closest of friends, and although the minister prayed fervently for Franklin's soul, he "never had the satisfaction of believing that his prayers were heard."[22] He did, however, have an effect in other ways on the statesman's life. He helped prepare Franklin to become a leader of the Revolution by convincing him that the thirteen American colonies were all part of God's plan for a specific purpose in history. Franklin was a confessed deist, who believed that God is revealed best through reason and personal experience, rather than in any supernatural way. While God created the universe, deists say that He then stepped aside to allow humans to manage things for themselves. Religion was a means to the end of being a truly useful human being whose life is geared toward bettering society. Although never a professing Christian, Franklin was nonetheless influenced by classic Christianity in much of his thought, including his beliefs about life after death. In a letter of condolence to his niece after her stepfather died, he demonstrated a belief in life beyond the grave, although he did not specify how a person could reach the immortal state he described. Perhaps he wasn't sure himself, but merely hopeful. He wrote:

Dear Miss Hubbard:

I condole with you. We have lost a most dear and valuable relation. But it is the will of God and nature, that these mortal bodies be laid aside, when the soul is to enter into real life. This is rather an embryo state, a preparation for living.

A man is not completely born until he is dead. Why then should we grieve, that a new child is born among the immortals, a new member added to their happy society? We are spirits. That bodies should be lent us, while they can afford us pleasure, assist us in acquiring knowledge, or in doing good to our fellow creatures, is a kind and benevolent act of God. When they become unfit for these purposes, and afford us pain instead of pleasure, instead of an aid become an encumbrance, and answer none of the intentions for which they were given, it is equally kind and benevolent, that a way is provided by which we may get rid of them. Death is that way. . . .

Our friend and we were invited abroad on a party of pleasure, which is to last for ever. His chair was ready first, and he is gone before us. We could not all conveniently start together; and why should you and I be grieved at this, since we are soon to follow, and know where to find him?[23]

࿎ↄoↄ࿎

As a result of the Great Awakening, church attendance boomed in the colonies. In addition, the moral tone of the day improved vastly, and there was a breaking down of barriers between people of various denominations and regions as they labored as equals in Christ's vineyard. Mission-mindedness and public service increased, especially in ministries among the Native Americans, and new institutions of higher learning were created to prepare young men for pastoral work including Princeton, Brown, Rutgers, and Dartmouth Universities. This outpouring of God's Spirit also led people to identify with "America," and not just a certain colony.

Many pastors gave their lives completely to help populate heaven and steal from hell, among them George Whitefield. Between 1736 and 1770 he delivered roughly eighteen thousand sermons in the American colonies; in one six-week period he delivered one hundred messages, and in a five-month time frame, he covered nearly two thousand miles. He preached through exhaustion and severe illness because he passionately desired to introduce people to the living Christ, who had saved his own soul from the ravages of sin and death.[24] In September 1770 he went to

New Hampshire to speak, but asthma made him barely able to breathe. A local pastor observed that there was no way Whitefield would be able to preach. In response, with a look toward heaven, Whitefield prayed, "Lord Jesus, I am weary *in* Thy work, but not *of* it. If I have not finished my course, let me go and speak for Thee once more in the fields, and seal Thy truth, and come home and die!"[25]

At first, when Whitefield rose to address the population of Exeter and its environs, he rambled breathlessly. After a brief pause, however, he told the people that he was waiting upon God's help, certain that it would come one more time. Then he went on to preach strongly, powerfully for two hours. The Rev. Jonathan Parsons noted, "He had such a sense of the incomparable excellencies of Christ that he could never say enough of Him."[26] As dawn broke the following morning, Whitefield died. His basic message, in fact the basic message of the Great Awakening, can be summed up by his words: "You, who are under the sense of sin, who are in fear of hell, if you seek unto your own works, you only seek your own death; for there is no fitness in you. I speak the truth in Christ Jesus, I lie not, there is not fitness in you, but a fitness for eternal damnation; for what are you by nature, but children of wrath, and your hearts are Satan's garrison."[27]

YOU SAY YOU WANT A
REVOLUTION

Today's celebrity-driven media exerts more influence on American life than any other institution. We care deeply about what the rich and famous say and do, believe and buy. During the period of the Revolutionary War, the citizens were also interested in the lives of the standard bearers, but there were differences between then and now. Over two hundred years ago, people looked up to those who stood out because of their strong Christian faith and morals. Instead of television, print media, and the Internet, the Protestant church was *the* force to be reckoned with, the primary trendsetter of standards and ethics. If someone disagreed with its principles and positions, he still had to come to terms with them because they shaped the way everyone lived. This filtered down all the way to the manner in which children were taught the alphabet in the leading textbook of the time, *The New England Primer*. Using Christianity and the Bible as its source of authority, the reader employed the following technique to teach both the gospel message of salvation in Christ and the alphabet:

A In ADAM'S Fall
We sinned all.

B Heaven to find;
The BIBLE Mind.

C CHRIST crucify'd
For sinners dy'd.

D The DELUGE drown'd
The Earth around.

E ELIJAH hid
By Ravens fed.

F The judgment made
FELIX afraid.[1]

Most early Americans owned two books, if they had any at all, the Bible and *The Pilgrim's Progress* by John Bunyan. There were newspapers, but most of them were only four pages long and contained dated information. Few colonial papers had any significant circulation. What most of the citizens read in terms of printed material were sermons. According to Peter Lillback, "In colonial culture with limited communication, besides word of mouth, the printed sermon was as influential as *Time* magazine is today. Sermons were one of the few printed publications."[2] Clearly, most Americans at that time were profoundly committed to Christian principles, and the people they admired were as well, especially the Founding Fathers who initiated the revolution against Great Britain.

Included among the Founding Fathers were the men who created the Declaration of Independence, the Articles of Confederation, and the Constitution—men such as George Washington, Thomas Jefferson, James Madison, and John Hancock. There also were "Founding Mothers," the women who most influenced Revolutionary American life and who often were connected to the male Founders, including Benjamin Franklin's wife, Deborah Read; John Adams's spouse, Abigail Adams; her friend Mercy Otis Warren; and Eliza Pinckney. Virtually all of them were Protestants with a strong faith. Even those who did not subscribe wholly to the Apostles' Creed, a main standard of orthodoxy, still had strong Christian convictions.[3] These were men and women on a mission, those of whom Martin Marty said, "They set out consciously to create an *empire* and, despite their great diversities, knew considerable success. They set out to attract the allegiance of all the people, to develop a spiritual kingdom, and to shape the nation's ethos, mores, manners, and often its laws."[4] They believed that God had called them to create a new nation based on the liberty that is found in Christian principles and that if they failed, they would be accountable to Him.

∽o∾

We look upon these figures today in hindsight, from the perspective of victory won more than sacrifices made, but sacrifice they did. They were able to cope as well as they did because of their conviction that they were engaged in a cosmic struggle between good and evil, heaven and hell, and because even if they lost everything, they would gain an eternal home with God. When news of the Declaration of Independence spread through the colonies, Massachusetts delegate John Adams wrote to his wife about the joy he felt in being present at the birth of a new nation, conceived in liberty, devoted to the conviction that before God all are equal. He knew, however, that the cost of breaking with England would be high: "It is the will of heaven that the two countries should be sundered forever. It may be the will of heaven that America shall suffer calamities still more wasting and distresses yet more dreadful."[5] Time would prove how much of that suffering would come upon his own family, especially Abigail.

As ardent a patriot as her husband, Mrs. Adams endured almost constant separation from him during the entire Revolutionary War period. She once wrote to a friend after a brief visit with him, "I find I am obliged to summon all my patriotism to feel willing to part with him again. You will readily believe me when I say that I make no small sacrifice to the public."[6] In the style of a single parent, she stayed behind to care for their four children, along with aging and sick relatives. She endured the death of a stillborn child in 1777, alone. Abigail once described her husband's absence as a "craveing void."[7] Both patriotism and faith in Christ sustained her during those difficult years, especially her firm belief that only Christian righteousness could exalt a nation. She also felt prepared to make the ultimate sacrifice for the country, if necessary, because Something even greater lay ahead. Of that she wrote, "If the Sword be drawn I bid adieu to all domestick felicity, and look forward to the Country where there is neither wars nor rumors of War in a firm belief that thro the mercy of its King we shall both rejoice there together."[8]

Abigail Adams constantly drilled into her children that God is life's only certainty and that He must come before everything else. We can see to just what extent she believed this in a letter to her son John Quincy—one that it is hard to imagine someone writing today:

> Improve your understanding for acquiring useful knowledge and virtue, such as will render you an ornament to society, an Honour to your Country and a Blessing to your parents. Great Learning and superior abilities, should you ever possess them, will be of little value and small Estimation, unless Virtue, Honour, Truth and integrity are added to them. Adhere to those religious Sentiments and principles which were early instilled into your mind and remember that you are accountable to your Maker for all your words and actions. Let me injoin it upon you to attend constantly and steadfastly to the precepts and instructions of your Father as you value the happiness of your Mother and your own welfare. . . . I had much rather you should have found your Grave in the ocean you have crossd or any untimely death crop you in your Infant years, rather than see you an immoral profligate or a Graceless child.[9]

～◦～

For most of the population the Revolution brought its share of trials—economic privation, British occupation, outbreaks of deadly diseases, a lack of creature comforts as basic as tea, and the heartbreak of sending loved ones off to battle. Americans called upon their deepest reserves of tenacity and faith, including the encouragement of Paul's words to the Roman church: "I consider that our present sufferings are not worth comparing with the glory that will be revealed in us" (Romans 8:18). In a July 3, 2000, article for *The Jewish World Review*, Jeff Jacoby wrote about the myriad sacrifices made by those who pledged their lives, fortunes, and sacred honor when they signed the Declaration of Independence that set the colonies on the path to war. He said:

> We tend to forget that to sign the Declaration of Independence was to commit an act of treason—and the punishment for treason was death. To publicly accuse George III of "repeated injuries and usurpations," to announce that Americans were therefore "Absolved from all Allegiance to the British Crown," was a move fraught with danger—so much so that the names of the signers were kept secret for six months. They were risking everything, and they knew it. . . .
>
> Most of the signers survived the war; several went on to illustrious careers. Two of them became presidents of the United States, and among the others were future vice presidents, senators, and governors. But not all were so fortunate.
>
> Nine of the 56 died during the Revolution, and never tasted American independence.
>
> Five were captured by the British.
>
> Eighteen had their homes—great estates, some of them—looted or burnt by the enemy.
>
> Some lost everything they owned.
>
> Two were wounded in battle. Two others were the fathers of sons killed or captured during the war.[10]

They were badly outnumbered by the world's greatest army and ill equipped, but they knew their Bibles and that in God's Word it plainly said that God's battles belong to Him. Like David who faced the seemingly invincible Goliath, they remembered his outcome and took courage that they, too, were doing the Lord's work.

No one knew better than George Washington how poor the chances of winning the war were apart from God's help. Elected Commander in Chief of the Continental Army in 1775 by the Second Continental Congress, he endured six grueling years of war as he led an army chronically low on supplies, and often low in spirits. The Congress frequently ignored his pleas for help or responded to them by sending a supply of virtually useless paper money. It seemed there never were enough recruits, and the superior British army badly outnumbered his ragtag collection. At Valley Forge, he presided over depleted ranks that suffered hunger and nakedness; one in four of those men succumbed to disease and exposure that winter.[11] He, too, suffered, wondering how the men would ever get through the winter with so little food and clothing. That February, John Joseph Stoudt, a civilian, wrote in his diary:

> For some days there has been little less than a famine in the camp. . . . Naked and starving as they are, we cannot enough admire the incomparable patience and fidelity of the soldiery, that they have not been excited ere this by their suffering, to a general mutiny and dispersion. Indeed, the distress of this army for want of provisions is perhaps beyond anything you can conceive.[12]

According to Peter Marshall and David Manuel, "The reason they endured—the reason they believed in God's deliverance—was simple: they could believe, because their General *did* believe."[13] Henry Muhlenberg, a Lutheran pastor at that time, said of Washington,

> His Excellency General Washington rode around among his army yesterday and admonished each and every one to fear God, to put away the wickedness that has set in and become so general, and to practice the Christian virtues. . . . The Lord God has also singularly, yea, marvelously, preserved him from harm in the midst of countless perils, ambuscades, fatigues, etc., and has hitherto graciously held him in His hand as a chosen vessel.[14]

And Isaac Potts, a Quaker whose home became Washington's headquarters at Valley Forge, once came upon the General on his knees in prayer, near his tethered horse. When he got home, Potts told his wife, "If George Washington be not a man of God, I am greatly deceived—and still more shall I be deceived, if God do not, through him, work out a great salvation for America."[15]

In May of that next welcome spring, the French entered the war on America's side, creating a sense of great hope and anticipation for the Continental Army. When Washington made the announcement to his troops, he reminded them that their prayers had been answered, that deliverance had come from God Himself, and that it was time to give thanks in a proper manner:

> It having pleased the Almighty Ruler of the universe to defend the cause of the United American States, and finally to raise up a powerful friend among the princes of the earth, to establish our liberty and independence upon a lasting foundation, it becomes us to set apart a day for gratefully acknowledging the divine goodness, and celebrating the important event, which we owe to His divine interposition.[16]

൞ഠൟ

In the days after July 4, 1776, Abigail Adams recorded that she was unafraid of what lay ahead in spite of the odds against the former colonists:

> I feel no great anxiety at the large armyment designed against us. The remarkable interpositions of Heaven in our favour cannot be too gratefully acknowledged. He who fed the Israelites in the wilderness, who cloaths the lilies of the Field and feeds the young Ravens when they cry, will not forsake a people engaged in so righteous a cause if we remember his Loving Kindness.[17]

Likewise, many pastors confidently told their congregations that God meant for the war to take place because of His divine purposes. One of them, Abraham Keteltas, explained what was happening in cosmic terms, saying, "The cause of truth, against error and falsehood . . . the cause of pure and undefiled religion, against bigotry, superstition, and human invention . . . in short, it is the cause of heaven against hell—of the kind Parent of the Universe against the prince of darkness, and the destroyer of the human race."[18] In that spirit, Americans faced the uncertain future, knowing that a greater place awaited them if they put their faith in Jesus Christ. Just what did they believe about the life to come, however? Peter Lillback says, "All the ranges of theological views were being heard then," including a Calvinism that emphasized God's coming stern judgement on His enemies. The circuit-riding ministers preached about the lostness of people apart from Christ and urged repentance, and there were also those whom Lillback refers to as "evangelical universalists," those Christians who hoped that ultimately God's grace would embrace everyone.[19] Among those was Benjamin Rush, a physician and signer of the Declaration of Independence. Although there were some variations according to different theological traditions, virtually all Americans agreed that there was a God, and most believed that His Son, Jesus Christ, came in human form to redeem the world from its fallen state. In addition, Christians across denominational lines understood that there was going to be a coming judgement, and the destiny of all souls was to be heaven or hell, depending on whether or not the person was saved.

So seriously did people take these views that they sometimes shunned those who came out on the wrong side of orthodox belief. Thomas Paine had written *Common Sense*, the popular pamphlet that urged Americans to declare independence. When he died in 1809, however, his caretakers couldn't find a place to bury him because he had been a "hard deist." "No one wanted him," says Lillback. He "not only denied that God had revealed himself in scripture, but he also denied that God acts in history."[20] Paine didn't believe in divine revelation or the incarnation of the "Word of God made flesh" in Jesus Christ. He wasn't completely without faith, however; he did believe in a Creator who also was to be the judge of man's destiny. Nevertheless, in the eyes of early-nineteenth-century America, Paine didn't warrant a Christian interment. He was finally laid to rest at his farm in New Rochelle, New York, and the site became badly neglected over the years. A decade later, an Englishman had Paine's bones dug up in an unsuccessful effort to give the man a proper burial in England, but he couldn't get enough support for his effort. No one knows what became of the patriot's body.

ALTERNATE
LIFESTYLES

They were countercultural and antiestablishment, men and women who lived by their own rules, apart from mainstream American life. They often made a living with their hands, creating arts and crafts, new products and techniques, as well as farming the communes in which they lived. Many of these freethinkers practiced open marriage, while others didn't consider marriage necessary. They championed causes and at times provoked violence among nonbelievers. In breaking from treasured societal norms, they set out to reinvent everything from fashions to families.

These radicals also revised cherished church teachings according to their own understanding of God and Jesus, which they considered to be higher and purer than what came from conventional pulpits. There were, however, communes that did not observe any religion at all, considering it to be antithetical to human progress. The former often tried to prepare the way for the second coming of Jesus and the hereafter by perfecting themselves and, in so doing, hoped to bring along most of American society. The latter attempted to create heaven on earth.

Perhaps this evokes a mental image of a bell-bottom-wearing individual sporting long, unwashed hair, love beads, fringe, tie-dyed T-shirt, and sandals, accompanied by such words as "hippie," "Jesus Freak," "Woodstock," and "Haight-Ashbury." That is the right framework, but the wrong era. The first countercultural Americans didn't arrive in the

1960s or '70s, but proliferated in the first part of the nineteenth century. The Janis Joplin, "Jesus Christ Superstar" generation may have seemed avant-garde at the time, but the truth is, they were far from original. They were preceded by more than a hundred years by other revolutionaries who could still manage to raise a few eyebrows today.

∽∘∾

When the first colonists came to America, most of them were out to become a city on a hill for all the world to see and follow as they practiced their faith freely and told the native inhabitants about Jesus Christ. That they achieved this dream on many points over the next century and a half, including America's defeat of the world's strongest army, led some to believe there was nothing Americans couldn't accomplish this side of heaven, including bringing heaven to earth. In the aftermath of the American Revolution, many utopian groups formed with the goal of perfecting individuals and society. Christianity inspired most of them, but they were anything but theologically orthodox or conventional. In fact, most of them came "preaching another gospel" (Galatians 1:8).

"Backwoods Utopias" peaked between 1820 and the 1840s. They were communal and experimental with many varieties and expressions, but they were mostly united in their quest for the perfection of society.[1] Sydney Ahlstrom views them as experiments controlled by charismatic leaders who were most often "anticlerical freethinkers and Christian enthusiasts."[2] "Almost by definition," he says, "the innovators rejected codes and statutes, traditions and customs—and this they did with more than usual abandon in the open society of the young American republic. In many cases they not only founded new sects, but called them out of the world."[3]

Their views about the afterlife varied with the teachings of their leaders, some of whom believed they were chosen by God to bring in the millennial kingdom as this world came to its conclusion. Most of these fringe groups embraced universalism in varying degrees, believing that somehow everyone makes it to heaven, even if it's a lesser manifestation of paradise than the true believer experiences.

One of America's earliest utopian communities went by the lofty title "The United Society of Believers in Christ's Second Coming" (the Millennial Church), but they are commonly known as the Shakers, a nickname given because of their energetic brand of worship.

Unlike the majority of radical groups that emerged in America's early days, a woman founded the Shakers, an English immigrant named Ann Lee Stanley. "Mother Ann" was a dynamo prone to trances and visions. She came to America with her husband, brother, and six followers in 1774 after convincing them that Christ would return as a woman—and, by the way, she was the one.[4] She believed that while Christ was the male manifestation of God, she was the deity's female expression; because of her belief in the duality of God, Mother Ann promoted equality between men and women. She maintained that neither Jesus nor she should be worshiped, however, but that both of them simply were elders in God's church. It was her job, she believed, to call people into lives of "blessedness" in this world in order to prepare for the next.

Beginning in Water Vliet, New York, and centered largely in that state as well as New England, the Shakers eventually branched out into Kentucky and Ohio. From 1830–1850 there were about six thousand followers in nineteen Shaker communities.[5] Mother Ann taught that sex was at the root of all sin and called her followers to celibacy; it wasn't necessary to procreate, she said, because "the Kingdom was literally at hand."[6] Shaker communities usually consisted of two "families" of about thirty individuals each that lived in large houses with the sexes rigidly segregated, using separate entrances, stairways, and sleeping quarters to avoid intermingling. Each family had two elders and two eldresses who were responsible for the spiritual management of the family. In order to join the Shakers, one had to engage in detailed oral confession of their sin, before witnesses, something that Mother Ann determined was necessary to attain salvation. In order to live apart from a corrupt society, they pursued self-sufficiency, with considerable success, creating economically viable communities.

The Shakers were spiritualists, believing that communication with the dead was possible, and they frequently held public seances. One Shaker apologist said, "We are thoroughly convinced of spirit communication and interpositions, spirit guidance and obsession. Our spiritualism has permitted us to converse, face to face, with individuals once mortals, some of whom we well knew, and with others born before the flood."[7]

According to Shaker beliefs, there is no original sin, no Trinity of the Godhead, nor was Jesus bodily resurrected from the dead. Their concept of heaven and hell was also more complicated than orthodox Protestantism. Shakers said there are four cycles of human history, with parallels in the spiritual world, and each of these has a heaven and hell. Noah and those living before the flood were in the first cycle, with Jews who lived up to the time of Christ in the second. The corresponding heaven for that period was known as Paradise. The third cycle consisted of people who came from then until the time of Ann Lee, and the fourth was still being worked out. Christ's kingdom had truly begun only with the founding of the Shaker church and would find its completion in it.[8] According to *The Shaker Manifesto*, "Those in the heavens and hells of our dispensation or degree may be gathered into the heavens of the succeeding dispensation or degree, as scholars may leave the ignorance, errors, and faults of one class, or school, by going up."[9] Elder Henry Clough's reasons for being a Shaker form a summary of that group's theology. He said, "I did not set out to obey the Gospel because I felt pressed with conviction for sin, not because I was afraid of going to hell, but because the requirements of the Gospel appeared to me as reasonable. I obeyed it from choice, to do that which was evidently right. I was drawn into it and kept in it by my love for that which was right and good."[10]

In the end, the Shaker kingdom never came, and they died out quickly because of their refusal to have children. Today, the Shakers are mainly remembered for their unique, eponymous style of furniture.

∽o∽

Another leading utopian experiment was the Oneida Community, founded in Putney, Vermont, in 1835 by John Humphrey Noyes. It is, however, mostly associated with the town of Oneida, New York, since the society eventually settled there. Noyes was a stormy man whose confrontations sometimes ended in his censure by those with whom he argued. Influenced by the preaching of Charles Finney, Noyes studied theology at Andover Theological Seminary and Yale Theological College. While at Andover, he recorded in his journal uneasy thoughts about his fitness for heaven and his fear of hell:

> July 29, Sabbath. My trouble for some days past has been this: I fear
> I think too much about the rewards of heaven. I seem to indulge
> an unhallowed ambition to stand eminent in the ranks of heaven,
> and I dislike the thought of death because it will cut me off from an
> opportunity of laying up a store of good works. This last feeling has given
> me especial trouble, because it is inconsistent with a perfect resignation
> to the will of God. I desire to feel, as I shall if I ever get to heaven, that it is
> a wonder if I escape hell. I shall think more of Christ then.[11]

In spite of his misgivings about his status before God, Noyes became convinced that human perfection was attainable in this life, and in 1834 while at Yale he announced publicly that he had become perfect. Authorities revoked his preaching license, and one can also imagine the guffaws and jeers of his classmates. He returned to his hometown where, two years later, he founded Putney Bible School, the Oneida community's forerunner.

Noyes taught that Christ could only return when people completely renounced sin. Somehow, communal ownership and "complex marriage" would help achieve that end. According to his rules, each man in his group was considered to be married to all of the women and vice-versa. Intermediaries arranged sexual encounters, and in a bid for equality, women were given veto power regarding their male partners. Members had to receive special permission to have babies. Noyes believed that marriage was for this life only, that there would be no need of it in heaven, one way in which his teachings approximated some semblance of orthodoxy.

Although he wanted to believe in universalism, he explained in a letter written in 1836 to Charles Weld why he could not. Perhaps he'd never fully abandoned the earlier evangelical influences on his life.

> If your will had been done, I should have been the bridge by which you and all the unclean in this world and in hell would have passed over into the Holy City, for the doctrine of universal salvation was evidently the ground of your own hope. But God will ere long remove from your mind as he has from mine every vestige of such a hope. You must drink the cup you have given me, and that eternally.[12]

The Oneida Community that Noyes created and personally oversaw consisted of about three hundred members. There also were five additional groups, in New Jersey, Vermont, New York, and Connecticut. Like the Shakers, members excelled in various industries, including the manufacture of silk thread and animal traps. (In the early twentieth century, Noyes's son Pierrepont shifted exclusively to the production of silverware, an enterprise that has endured.)

Noyes's later years brought further musings about this life and the one to come as he continued to develop his theology and his utopian community. In spite of other way-out positions, he maintained a classic view of hell as a pit, a place of horrors, and the only ones who would avoid it would be "'they that do his commandments' (who) may enter in through the gates into the city, and have the right to the fruit of the tree of life."[13]

In his youth, John Noyes ran afoul of church officials when he announced that he had reached a sinless state. In 1879, at the age of sixty-eight, he was still causing trouble. He escaped by night to Canada after someone alerted him that he was about to be arrested for statutory rape, hardly an illustrious ending for a man of his position. From his exile he wrote to instruct his community to abandon complex marriage and pursue a more conventional route. Five years before his death in 1886, the utopian Oneida Community dissolved, becoming a joint-stock company instead.

∽∘∾

Not all of the utopians pursued a theological agenda in the early decades of the nineteenth century. In fact, some envisioned a perfect society that had absolutely nothing to do with God, nor were they thinking in terms of heaven or hell. Robert Owen, the Welsh-born founder of New Harmony in Indiana, was a socialist whose beliefs embraced the principles of the Enlightenment and would draw the attention of Karl Marx. In his community, men and women held to common ownership, and children were raised apart from their parents. Owen believed that religion was "based on the same absurd imagination" that resulted in man's being "a weak, imbecile animal; a furious bigot and fanatic; or a miserable hypocrite."[14] Toward the end of his life, though, he became fascinated with spiritualism, claiming that he could communicate with great people of the past by means of electricity. His commune lasted three years, from 1825–28.

Another nonreligious communal experiment was the North American Phalanx, consisting of forty secular societies based on principles of the French utopian socialist Charles Fourier. He believed, among other things, that industrialization was but a passing phase in human history. With headquarters in Red Bank, New Jersey, where the movement began in 1844, its adherents asserted that poverty could be eliminated by establishing communities around scientific principles or "phalanxes," to be run like a joint-stock company. This group also practiced equality of the sexes. Most of the phalanxes were but a passing vapor, although one lasted for eighteen years.

There also was Frances "Fanny" Wright, who founded the Nashoba Colony in the mid-1820s near Memphis, Tennessee. She was a radical, an abolitionist who created an interracial group in which slaves received an education and enough money to work for their freedom so they could prepare for a better life in Haiti. Her ideas clashed with prevailing social mores, including her bold teachings that there should be no nuclear family or religion, as well as no private property or slavery. After she became ill with malaria and went to Europe to recover, the commune dissolved, just four years after its inception.

∽∘∾

Only one nineteenth-century communitarian group has survived according to its founding principles and, in fact, now boasts nearly twelve million members worldwide. The Church of Jesus Christ of Latter Day Saints (LDS) had its origins in 1820 in upstate New York when a fourteen-year-old boy went off to seek from God which church he should join. Joseph Smith said that at that time God the Father and Jesus appeared to him, revealing that the church started by Jesus had vanished, and it was up to Smith to restore it. He claimed that over the next ten years other heavenly messengers instructed him, a period in which he translated the Book of Mormon.

Like Noyes, Smith gave a great deal of thought to matters of the afterlife, which are elaborated in Mormon instructional books. According to their theology, there are three heavens: "The highest levels of the Celestial Kingdom are reserved for Mormon couples who have been married in a Mormon temple and thus have had their marriage sealed for eternity."[15] They can eventually become a god and goddess, with the husband being in control of an entire universe. In addition, "Christians who are non-Mormons and have led truly exceptional lives will also spend eternity in the Celestial Kingdom."[16]

The second, or Terrestrial, Kingdom is the destination for most individuals, while the Telestial Kingdom is reserved for "liars, and sorcerers, and adulterers, and whoremongers."[17] At death, individuals are assigned to one of the three Kingdoms for the purpose of learning and making spiritual progress.[18] Furthermore, "couples who are not sealed (married in a Mormon temple) will be automatically divorced at death and will spend eternity as single individuals."[19]

Mormons believe that while hell exists, very few people will spend eternity there. Instead, most will eventually "pass into the telestial kingdom; the balance, cursed as 'sons of perdition', will be consigned to partake of endless wo [sic] with the devil and his [fallen] angels."[20] "Sons of perdition" are defined as once-devout Mormons who have become apostates by rejecting God's truth by leaving the LDS church. While this appears to be the official teaching of the church, other Mormons have a broader definition that includes "persons who have knowingly committed very serious sins and have not repented and sought God's forgiveness—sins like murder and premarital sex.[21]

According to Mormonism, everyone will be resurrected, and unbelievers, the heathen, and children who die before reaching the age of discretion will all go to the Celestial Kingdom.[22] Additional benefits beyond simple resurrection will be gained by those who do good works.

Joseph Smith pressed ever westward with his followers, spreading his teachings and, at one point, even announcing a bid for the U.S. presidency. His belief in polygamy, along with his success in gathering large numbers of converts, so upset people in the mainstream that he kept getting kicked out of their towns and moving on. Mormonism's spread from New York to Utah is an epic saga that includes Smith's murder at the hands of a livid posse.

∾o∾

Each of the utopian leaders and his or her communities dreamed of bringing about permanent change in the world. None of them, however, lasted in any way directly connected to their original form, except for the Mormons. For the most part, these were misguided zealots who raised eyebrows, as well as the ire of the people where they lived, as they challenged and flaunted societal norms.

It is no wonder that they emerged where and when they did, in a new country with lofty principles, wide open to the highest dreams humanity is capable of dreaming, a place and a time in which old ways were giving way to new visions of a better world. Even so, most people in that era remained Protestant and orthodox in their convictions, committed to the Creator God and His rules for righteousness. In spite of their brevity or even kookiness, the utopian experiments opened up the national conversation, at first in small ways, to possibilities beyond the accepted and established in matters of life and death.

THAT OLD-TIME
RELIGION

I n the years just after the birth of the American republic, many people set out to conquer its vast frontier—risk-takers like Daniel Boone and George Rogers Clarke, as well as individuals in search of land and livelihood. There were also ministers who, above all, desired to care for the pioneers' souls. All of them faced daunting trials on the frontier such as primitive sanitation and roads, vulnerability to attacks from hostile Native Americans and lawless men, unpredictable weather, and terrible isolation. There were few schools or churches, and hardly any other trappings of civilization.

In the late 1790s, James McGready, a Presbyterian pastor, oversaw three small Kentucky congregations in Gasper River, Red River, and Muddy River, in addition to organizing camp meetings to minister to meet the religious needs of frontiersmen living long distances from their nearest neighbors. The outdoor meetings lasted for several days to allow settlers to come together away from their everyday hardships to receive fellowship and spiritual nurture. News of these assemblies spread by word of mouth from people who had been convicted by McGready's challenge to repent of their sins and accept Jesus Christ, and soon pioneers jammed the outdoor services. In July 1800, while he preached to his Gasper River congregation, McGready told them about the revival that had broken out during the camp meetings he'd just conducted. He remarked that many of those who attended had become convicted of not knowing Christ, even though they thought they were Christians. He said:

> It was truly affecting to see them lying powerless, crying for mercy, and
> speaking to their friends and relations, in such language as this: "O, we
> were deceived—I have no religion; I know now there is a reality in these
> things: three days ago I would have despised any person that would have
> behaved as I am doing now; but, O, I feel the very pains of hell in my
> soul." This was the language of a precious soul, just before the hour of
> deliverance came.[1]

The following year brought what one scholar has called the greatest
outpouring of the Holy Spirit since the day of Pentecost as McGready and
several other ministers preached at the Cane Ridge Revival in Kentucky.[2]
Although the clerics had anticipated a large crowd, even they were astounded by the turnout of between ten and twenty-five thousand people,
most who had come from great distances over treacherous roads. Sidney
Ahlstrom described one of those services with vivid imagery:

> One must first try to re-create the scene: the milling crowds of hardened
> frontier farmers, tobacco-chewing, tough-spoken, notoriously profane,
> famous for their alcoholic thirst; their scarcely demure wives and large
> broods of children; the rough clearing, the rows of wagons and crude
> improvised tents with horses staked out behind; the gesticulating
> speaker on a rude platform, or perhaps simply a preacher holding
> forth from a fallen tree. At night, when the forest's edge was limned by
> the flickering light of many campfires, the effect of apparent miracles
> would be heightened. For men and women accustomed to retiring and
> rising with the birds, these turbulent nights must have been especially
> awe-inspiring. And underlying every other conditioning circumstance
> was the immense loneliness of the frontier farmer's normal life and the
> exhilaration of participating in so large a social occasion.[3]

The Cane Ridge Revival was nothing if not dramatic, including times
when rowdy detractors would suddenly fall under conviction of sin and
collapse "'as suddenly as if struck by lightning,' sometimes at the very
moment they were cursing the proceedings."[4] The meetings went on

day and night without letup, and those who were converted often capti-
vated the preachers by giving their own gripping testimonies. At times
the shouts of the people repenting were so great that they could be heard
for miles.⁵ These services marked the beginning of the country's Second
Great Awakening, a revival that "would spread through the gaps and
over the turnpikes and down the rivers—wherever men traveled, whose
lives had been profoundly altered by what happened in Kentucky."⁶ It
persisted throughout the nineteenth century in various ways and times,
dominating and defining American culture. One of its dominant aspects
was an emphasis on heaven and hell, the latter of the fire and brimstone
variety. This was the essence of "that old-time religion."

✦

Throughout history it has been God's good pleasure to use improbable
conditions and unlikely people to reconcile the world to Himself. It is no
surprise, then, that a major movement of His Spirit in the United States
began in Evans Mills, New York. Its citizens liked their preachers to be as
they were, conservative and reserved, very much status quo. The Wom-
en's Missionary Society of Western New York sent them a steady supply
of temporary pastors who came for a few months at a time, delivering
sermons in the schoolhouse that doubled as a church on the Sabbath. The
most notable was Charles Finney, a lawyer and native of Litchfield, Connecticut, who had undergone a powerful experience of God's presence in
1821 while reading the Bible. He soon took up preaching, managing to
upset the educated clergy with his bluntness and unconventionally fervent delivery. He was known to "preach at" people in the audience, for
example, piercing them with his eyes as his six-foot-plus frame towered
over them. Finney didn't seem to care much about other people's opinions of him, a quality that he took to Evans' Mills in 1824.

At first Finney preached before small and polite gatherings at the
church, but he quickly became impatient with their lack of an earnest
response to his trenchant sermons about sin and salvation. During one

evening service he issued an ultimatum: "I won't stay here another day unless you repent and receive Christ. State your intention by standing." The people were so stunned by the strange exhortation that no one moved, let alone stood. Finney shouted at them, "Then you are committed! You have rejected Christ and his Gospel, and ye are witnesses one against the other, and God is witness against you all!"[7]

The people weren't used to such a display, and they demanded that Finney explain himself. He refused. After several minutes, the minister said he would return the next night to speak to them once more. The majority of the town, including the most committed of the believers, believed he'd gone way too far, except for one man who told Finney he thought he'd given them exactly what they needed.[8] All the next afternoon those two men prayed together for God to guide the pastor, and that night a large crowd came to hear what he had to say for himself. Finney later recalled what happened:

> The Spirit of God came upon me with such power that it was like opening a battery upon them. For more than an hour . . . the word of God came through me to them in a manner that I could see was carrying all before it. It was a fire and a hammer breaking the rock, and the sword that was piercing to the dividing asunder of soul and spirit. I saw that a general conviction was spreading over the whole congregation. Many of them could not hold up their heads.[9]

One honorable woman who had considered herself a Christian for many years became convinced that she wasn't right with God after all, that she was actually bound for hell. Her subsequent conversion created a groundswell among the people toward Christ. The revival that proceeded in Evans' Mills swept many into the kingdom on waves of repentance, including a notorious saloon owner who turned his bar into a gathering place for prayer. The church and town, indeed much of western New York, moved from complacent to keen in their faith in what was one of the early and significant movements of the Holy Spirit in the Second Great Awakening.[10]

✌⌒∾

In both Great Awakenings there was an emphasis on sin and salvation, including the joys of heaven and the terrors of hell, subjects that got an ample hearing in those eras, albeit with some variations. Eighteenth-century revivalists had underscored the doctrine of predestination, that is, how God had chosen some for salvation and others for eternal punishment, but in the Second Great Awakening preachers focused more on the individual's responsibility to accept God's gift of salvation. For both movements, however, hell played a major role in getting people to turn away from sin and live for God. In a message based on Luke 16:2, Charles Finney warned the people that judgement awaited them:

> You must give an account for your soul. You have no right to go to hell. God has a right to your soul; your going to hell would injure the whole universe. It would injure hell, because it would increase its torments. It would injure heaven, because it would wrong it out of your services. Who shall take the harp in your place, in singing praises to God? Who shall contribute your share to the happiness of heaven?
>
> Do you still say, What if I do lose my soul, it is nobody's business but my own? That is false: it is every body's business. Just as well might a man bring a contagious disease into a city, and spread dismay and death all around, and say it was nobody's business but his own.[11]

Contemporary Americans are uncomfortable discussing hell at all, with many refusing to believe that a loving God would send anyone to such a grisly place. Finney, however, spoke boldly about hell with the hope that such plain speaking would usher as many people as possible away from it, and the public accepted his messages. He proclaimed in a sermon about the rich man and Lazarus from Luke 16:19–31:

> In all ages it has been common for some dying saints to hear music which they supposed to be of heaven and to see angels near and around them. With eyes that see what others cannot see, they recognize their attending angels as already come, "Don't you hear that music?" say they. "Don't

you see those shining ones? they come, they come!" . . . No doubt in such cases, they do really see angelic forms and hear angelic voices. The Bible says—"Precious in the sight of the Lord is the death of his saints." How gloriously do these closing scenes illustrate this truth.

If this be true of saints, then doubtless wicked spirits are allowed to drag the wicked down from their dying beds to hell. Nor is it unreasonable to suppose that they too really see awful shapes and hear dreadful sounds. "Who is that weeping and wailing? Did I not hear a groan? Is there not some one weeping as if in awful agony? O, that awful thing; take him away, take him away! He will seize me and drag me down; take him away, away!" . . .

Christian parents, one word to you. Suppose you conceive of this as your case. You see one of your children crying, "O give me one drop of water to cool my burning tongue!" I know what Universalists would say to this. They say, "Can a parent be happy, and see this? And do you think a parent is more compassionate than God?"

But in that hour of retribution, those Christian parents will say even of the sons and daughters they have borne, "Let them perish, they are the enemies of God and of his kingdom! Let them perish, since they would not have salvation! They must perish, for God's throne must stand and ought to stand, though all the race go down to hell!"[12]

⌀⌀⌀

A stereotype exists of men like Finney as rough-hewn preachers breathing hellfire and brimstone sermons about eternal punishment, but concern and passion about hell weren't limited to such men. In that era, many well-educated, socially polished pastors also addressed the issue with ardor. Among them was Timothy Dwight, the elegant grandson of no less a figure than Jonathan Edwards. In 1795, Dwight became the eighth president of Yale, and from his first day in office, he confronted a spirit of "infidelity" that he discerned among the students and faculty. Lyman Beecher, who would go on to be another leader in the Second Great Awakening, was a student at the time. He agreed with his new president's assessment: "Before he came, college was in a most ungodly state. The college church was almost extinct. Most of the students were skeptical."[13]

Dwight fired faculty members who advocated the rationalist philosophy of the anti-Christian French Revolution, and then he began having individual conversations with the students, asking them to be honest about their beliefs, and their disbelief. As he preached to them about the dangers of unfaithfulness to Christ, the Spirit began moving among them, bringing many to repentance. By 1802 a revival had broken out, leading to the conversion of half of the student body, a movement that lasted for many years on that campus. A characteristic of the movement was Dwight's candor about what it meant to be lost. In one baccalaureate address, he gave the illustration of a young man named Lorenzo, who came to Yale from a good family but who fell into a cycle of selfish, lawless living. He often ridiculed Christ and the idea of a future judgment, and after graduating he no longer attended church or read the Bible. He eventually lost his inheritance, and his mother died broken in spirit. He was despised in his community. The profligate died young and on his deathbed he "then, too late . . . thought, with horror, of death and the eternal torments of hell, and wished he might live to repent." As Dwight concluded, he asked the students, "Which of you, my young friends, would wish to be Lorenzo?"[14]

Dwight and other revivalists believed that a person had to have a strong conviction of his own sinfulness and lost state. Once that happened, he could then "properly appreciate the greatness of his deliverance, the goodness of God in rescuing him, or the nature of that happiness to which he was to gain final admission. It was a necessary preparation for heaven."[15] Accounts flowed from Yale of students who writhed in their spirits for days as they considered the lostness of their souls and the anguish of hell. In one case, a young man became terribly ill:

> Every day increased his sense of the coming wrath of God. The approach
> of night seemed to him like the approach of the day of judgment. One
> evening, a few Christian friends lingered about his bed, offering prayers

for his sanctification. Finally, one went for Dr. Dwight, fearing that unless the boy had some relief, death itself might ensue. The messenger was Asahel Nettleton, who became a prominent itinerant revivalist in his mature years. The hour was late, but Dwight came promptly. For a short time he seemed overwhelmed, sharing deeply in the youth's agony. Taking a seat by the bedside, he recited the invitations of the gospel, and followed his parental counsel with a prayer to God. That prayer, they believed, was heard. "A sweet serenity" seemed to steal over the agitated sinner's mind, a serenity which was the harbinger of a joy which came a short time after. He gained the hope he so much wanted.[16]

It's difficult to imagine a modern American college president guiding his students through such gritty spiritual experiences, but Dwight was concerned about their salvation above all other earthly considerations. He saw nothing as more important to their education and development.

∽∘∾

It's been commonly said that sometimes the people of God are so heavenly minded that they're no earthly good, but Charles Finney would have ridiculed such an idea. His zeal for saving souls was matched by his conviction that the redeemed of the Lord had a sacred obligation to fix a broken society. In a sermon about stewardship, he outlined his position:

> The world is full of poverty, desolation, and death; hundreds and millions are perishing, body and soul; God calls on you to exert yourself as his steward, for their salvation; to use all the property in your possession, so as to promote the greatest possible amount of happiness among your fellow-creatures. The Macedonian cry comes from the four winds of heaven, "Come over and help us;" COME OVER AND HELP US; and yet you refuse to help; you hoard up the wealth in your possession, live in luxury, and let your fellow-men go to hell. What language can describe your guilt?[17]

The Second Great Awakening ushered in a century in which Christians led the charge against all kinds of social evils, including ignorance, poverty, poor work conditions, and the wretched lot of the mentally ill, the deaf, the blind, and prisoners. "These crusades and the people behind them created a momentum that persisted throughout the century."[18] One prominent preacher who promoted social activism was Lyman Beecher, a Presbyterian minister who had studied under Timothy Dwight at Yale. Like other leaders in the Second Great Awakening, Beecher preached often and ardently about heaven and hell, often linking the latter with the evils of alcohol consumption, a scourge to many American families. In fact, the attack against "demon rum" was the most popular of all nineteenth-century social reform movements. Widespread drunkenness was the norm, and people who imbibed often started their day with hard cider for breakfast. In 1820 the per capita consumption of hard liquor was five gallons a year, the highest in American history, with families suffering the consequences.[19] Lyman Beecher led the early temperance movement, and in one of his sermons on the subject, he linked the issue to hell itself:

> But of all the ways to hell, which the feet of deluded mortals tread, that of the intemperate is the most dreary and terrific. The demand for artificial stimulus to supply the deficiencies of healthful aliment, is like the rage of thirst, and the ravenous demand of famine. It is famine: for the artificial excitement has become as essential now to strength and cheerfulness, as simple nutrition once was. But nature, taught by habit to require what once she did not need, demands gratification now with a decision inexorable as death, and to most men as irresistible. The denial is a living death. The stomach, the head, the heart, and arteries, and veins, and every muscle, and every nerve, feel the exhaustion, and the restless, unutterable wretchedness which puts out the light of life, and curtains the heavens, and carpets the earth with sackcloth.[20]

Beecher also championed the abolition of slavery, a cause that many Christians took up in mid-century, one that was as divisive as abortion is today. Among those who helped bring about the emancipation of the slaves was Harriet Beecher Stowe, who became inspired to write a story about the evils of that institution while listening to a sermon one Sunday morning. She felt the sufferings of those in bondage so keenly that she wrote the stirring, controversial novel *Uncle Tom's Cabin*. It caused so much furor in both the North and the South that some felt it ignited the Civil War.

Another prominent Christian abolitionist, in fact the one who helped bring respectability to the movement, was Elijah Lovejoy, a Presbyterian pastor who died defending his printing press in Alton, Illinois. His publication of an abolitionist newspaper had so enraged some people that they destroyed his three earlier presses, but he persisted, saying:

> You have courts and judges and juries; they find nothing against me. And now you come together for the purpose of driving out a confessedly innocent man, for no cause but that he dares to think and speak his conscience as his God dictates. . . . You may hang me up as the mob hung up the individuals at Vicksburg. You may burn me at the stake, as they did McIntosh at St. Louis. . . . I shall not flee away from Alton. Should I attempt it, I would feel that the angel of the Lord with his flaming sword was pursuing me wherever I went . . . the contest has commenced here, and here it must be finished. . . . The deepest of all disgrace would be, at a time like this, to deny my Master by forsaking His cause. . . . If I fall, my grave shall be made in Alton.[21]

One effect of Christian activism during the Second Great Awakening was the growing involvement of women in social affairs. Prior to that time, it was considered improper for women to speak publicly, but this gradually began to change when Charles Finney encouraged women to pray during his revivals. He believed that giving women a greater voice would help them use their gifts from God toward saving souls and changing what was wrong with the world. As a result, women like Sarah and Angelina Grimke, Frances Willard, and Phoebe Palmer became leading Christian social reformers of the nineteenth century. Former slaves Harriet Tubman and Sojourner Truth also spoke out against slavery and for women's rights from public platforms with the support of leading men of the day.

The Second Great Awakening's profound contribution to the betterment of American life throughout the nineteenth century and beyond is difficult to measure. It was a time in which to be a Christian meant that one necessarily got involved in changing people's destinies from here to eternity. This was what it meant to them to be redeemed. In addition, the decades-long revival reinforced orthodox beliefs, and vivid imagery about heaven and hell—descriptions so seared into the nation's consciousness that they would endure for generations.

KNOCKING ON HEAVEN'S DOOR

In the middle part of the nineteenth century, America's urge to make the world a better place remained undaunted, the outlook for human and technological progress was bright, and the appetite for exploration persisted. Still, the people lived in the shadow of death. Life expectancy had fallen dramatically, from age fifty-six in 1790 to just forty-eight in 1860. Major diseases such as typhoid, scarlet fever, and tuberculosis cut down lives, often with a terrifying suddenness.[1] Understanding of those maladies was at a practically medieval level, and as Americans became increasingly mobile, they came into contact with a variety of illnesses that they had not encountered before. In addition, childhood mortality was high, with one in every five infants born not making it to their first birthday.[2]

Then there was the devastation wrought by the Civil War. Nicholas Marshall researched diaries of the period, along with correspondence, discovering that they were "saturated with discussions of affliction. Constant illness and frequent death were the most significant elements in the lives of the common people, far outweighing any other concerns."[3] Curiously, while those Americans lived in the midst of such unrelenting harshness, they began to perceive God differently—more benevolently than in previous times. During the first wave of revivals a hundred years earlier, they tended to think of God dangling them like helpless spiders over the chasm of hell, who would gladly drop them into it were it not for

Christ's intervention on the cross. One could only hope, strict Calvinists believed, that God had chosen them for the halls of heaven. According to the teachings of most Second Great Awakening preachers, however, people were free agents who could make a decision for or against Christ. It's not that they no longer thought of hell and damnation, but they maintained that it was up to individuals to choose their eternal destiny. Of course, only a fool or reprobate would take the path to hell, they reasoned.

Since they couldn't rely on doctors to cure their diseases, and they didn't have much more than folk remedies to provide relief, where did Americans turn for solace? Most appealed to God. A Christian worldview dominated American thought, and it was "Christian, predominantly Protestant, ideas" that informed their thinking about life and death.[4] By that time, Americans were becoming more sentimental in their outlook and their relationships. Nicholas Marshall discovered that it was Christianity that provided the main support system for people, including a kinder and gentler view of God. He said:

> Americans . . . increasingly viewed Christianity as a support to be
> relied on during seemingly never-ending cycles of emotional distress.
> Traditional doctrines of predestination could not be sustained, and so a
> new, more sympathetic religion was replacing the older one. No longer
> was God's main purpose to divide humankind into saved and damned
> (with only a small portion thought to be in the former category). Instead,
> God chose to suffuse the society with love and care in an effort to save
> all that could be saved. The ultimate goal for Christians was to find their
> place in a domesticated heaven. As long as they were prepared—having
> experienced saving grace—all loved ones would be reunited in a heaven,
> as so many put it, "where parting is no more." The drone of physical and
> emotional pain, taking its toll in daily life, would finally be overcome in
> this soothing afterlife.[5]

People often became Christians in response to their suffering, finding peace and strength for today and a bright hope for tomorrow in their faith. Increasingly, they saw themselves as having a say in the matter, unlike the severe Calvinism of an earlier era. Along with that new mind-set came more of an accent on the joys of heaven, which included reunions with loved ones, than the terrors of hell. This was a major shift that had begun a century earlier when Emmanuel Swedenborg published his views about heaven. Distinctly anthrocentric, this heaven was a place where earthly existence was continued, but on a higher plane, including the continuation of the love people had known on earth. This perspective peaked in the mid-nineteenth century, and into the opening years of the twentieth.[6] Prior to this time in Western Christianity, the emphasis was on intimacy with God in the afterlife.

∽o∾

A heartbreaking fact of life during this time was the helplessness parents often felt when their children became ill and died. Just as there had been a shift over the previous few decades in terms of how Americans viewed God and heaven, so their perception of childhood had also changed. Children were no longer as necessary as they once had been to the household economy, and middle-class parents were beginning to regard them—and childhood itself—in a more sentimental way. This created a "delicate balancing act as they attempted to hold their children loosely and at God's disposal."[7] Examples abound. In Louisa May Alcott's semiautobiographical novel *Little Women*, the author tells the tender story of Beth, the most spiritual of the March sisters. After selflessly ministering to a desperately poor German family, she contracted smallpox and nearly died. Although she survived, her heart was so weakened that she only lived a few more years. On her deathbed she exuded confidence and joy about going to heaven, inspiring her sister Jo to become more like her, and to look forward to someday being reunited with Beth in the hereafter.

American literature was full of such stories, including the bestselling novel *The Wide, Wide World* by Susan Bogert Warner. A deeply sentimental work, the novel struck historian J. C. Furnas as a "massive bouquet of deathbed scenes."[8] These books weren't meant just to entertain, but to demonstrate how faithful Christians should face the last enemy. In one chapter of *The Wide, Wide World*, Warner tells the story of Alice as she prepared to die:

> Still her greatest comfort was Ellen. Her constant thoughtful care; the thousand tender attentions, from the roses daily gathered for her table to the chapters she read and the hymns she sung to her; the smile that often covered a pang; the pleasant words and tone that many a time came from a sinking heart; they were Alice's daily and nightly cordial. . . .
>
> Mr. Humphreys came in often to see his daughter, but never stayed long. It was plain he could not bear it. It might have been difficult too for Alice to bear, but she wished for her brother. She reckoned the time from Mrs. Chauncey's letter to that when he might be looked for; but some irregularities in the course of the post-office made it impossible to count with certainty upon the exact time of his arrival. Meanwhile her failure was very rapid. Mrs. Vawse began to fear he would not arrive in time. . . .
>
> One morning when Ellen went into her room, Alice drew her close to her and said, "You remember, Ellie, in the *Pilgrim's Progress*, when Christiana and her companions were sent to go over the river?—I think the messenger has come for me. You mustn't cry, love;—listen—this is the token he seems to bring me,—'I have loved thee with an everlasting love.' I am sure of it, Ellie; I have no doubt of it;—so don't cry for me. You have been my dear comfort, my blessing—we shall love each other in heaven, Ellie."[9]

In real life, author Harriet Beecher Stowe suffered the loss of her year-old son, Charley, to cholera, and she reconciled herself to this death by thinking of him as a "special child." She mused, "Is there a peculiar love given us for those that God wills to take from us? Is there not something brighter and better around them than around those who live—Why else in so many households is there a tradition of one brighter more beautiful more promising than all the rest, laid early low."[10] Author Nina Baym has said the idea that God had special children had "immense reconciling power in an era when many children did in fact die young."[11]

Although diseases that few understood claimed many lives, illness was not the only dreaded killer. By 1860, the valley of the shadow lengthened across a divided nation on the threshold of civil war.

⌇∞⌇

When Abraham Lincoln was elected president in 1860, the country was irreparably torn apart by sectional difficulties. A month after his inauguration in April, 1861 war broke out, and over the next four years, the nation's families endured catastrophic losses—of loved ones, homes, businesses, and farms. Among the North, 360,222 soldiers died, just over 67,000 of them in battle, another 43,000 from wounds, nearly a quarter of a million from diseases such as dysentery, malaria, typhoid, and consumption, and over 25,000 from accidents and other causes. Between 80,000 and 90,000 Confederate soldiers perished in battle, while disease claimed between 160,000 and 180,000 more.[12] With death such a frequent companion, Americans drew strength from their faith, and they had a sense of urgency about making sure their loved ones were prepared to meet their Maker on the right terms.

In this atmosphere, Americans were becoming more committed to a general, evangelical Christianity and less particular about denominational affiliations. Nonetheless, a belief in heaven and hell remained a firm feature, with thoughts of heaven providing relief for their emotional and physical distress. Many leading Civil War personalities subscribed to this state of belief, including General Ulysses S. Grant. Although he never formally joined a church, he identified himself as a Methodist. James L. Crane, who served as a chaplain under the Union officer, said:

> Grant belongs to no church organization, yet he entertains and
> expresses the highest esteem for all the enterprises that tend to promote
> religion. . . . While he was colonel of the Twenty-first Regiment he gave
> every encouragement and facility for securing a prompt and uniform
> observance of religious services, and was generally found in the audience
> listening to preaching.[13]

Grant's Confederate counterpart, Robert E. Lee, was a Christian who encouraged his men to have cross-denominational prayer meetings. On one occasion as he rode along, he noticed a group of soldiers praying, and he stopped. Dismounting, he removed his hat and stood among the men "in an attitude of profound respect and attention, while the earnest prayer proceeded, in the midst of the thunder of artillery and the explosions."[14] In May 1863, when Lee learned that Stonewall Jackson had been wounded at the Battle of Chancellorsville, he sent word to Jackson that he was praying for him: "When a suitable occasion offers, give him my love, and tell him that I wrestled in Prayer for him last night, as I never prayed, I believe, for myself."[15]

Thomas "Stonewall" Jackson had become a Christian while serving in the occupation army after the Mexican-American War. At the time, he was experiencing what would turn out to be a lifetime of stomach-related illnesses. He wrote about them in a letter to his sister, but not as a complaint. Rather, Jackson told her that he regarded the affliction as coming from "Heaven's sovereign" as a way of turning him from a life that he felt had been leading him straight to hell. Jackson said the illness was "a punishment for my offenses against his Holy Laws and have probably been the instrument of turning me from the path of eternal death, to that of everlasting life."[16] His conversion was deep and lasting, and he became known as a model of Christian character, as well as something of a Christian "character." During the Civil War, Jackson ordered the chaplains serving under him to conduct services of thanksgiving after each of their victories, and the General frequently distributed Christian tracts to his soldiers and participated in their worship times. The men under his command sometimes noticed Jackson stumbling around on his own, falling and picking himself up again, looking very drunk. They knew better. He was simply praying, with his eyes closed.[17] Jackson once said that he felt as safe in battle as he did in bed, that he had a peaceful assurance that God had appointed a certain day for his death. This reflected his very Presbyterian belief in the sovereignty of God. In May 1863, his own troops accidentally shot him, and eight days later, his time came. He accepted death calmly saying, "I always wanted to die on a Sunday."[18]

Other notable military figures who shared a strong devotion to Christ and urged their subordinates to put their faith in Him included William Pendleton, an Episcopal priest who became the Confederate artillery chief; Oliver O. Howard, dubbed "Old Prayer Book," who led his Northern brigade to a defeat at the First Battle of Bull Run, which he blamed on the Union Army's decision to strike on a Sunday; and General George B. McClellan, who came to Christ around the same time that he became commander of the Union Army in 1861. Agreeing with Howard that the first Bull Run disaster probably happened because they had attacked on the Sabbath, McClellan ordered that, whenever possible, Sunday be observed as the Lord's Day with religious services.

∽o∾

Besides the high-ranking military men, what of those serving under them? Did they give much thought to eternal matters as they slogged in and out of treacherous military campaigns, never knowing if or when the next bullet would have their name on it? In the initial weeks and months of the war, most of the soldiers were caught up in a cavalier attitude. They were young; they were going to live forever; they were going to teach the enemy a lesson. So thoughts of heaven and hell seemed remote for most of them. As the war began to drag on, however, many soldiers started to think about death and the afterlife. Chaplain Alan Farley, director of Re-Enactors Missions for Jesus Christ, says, "Seeing and experiencing the brutality of war brings a man to thoughts of eternity." He especially noted a revival that "swept through the Confederate army" that had men constantly confronting themselves with the question, "Are you ready to meet your maker?" Farley states, "I do believe it was a matter that many, not all of course, but a large number, gave serious thought about, and did something about."[19] It is interesting to note that when Ken Burns did his landmark documentary on the Civil War in 1990, he did not address the issue of how heaven and hell motivated, soothed, or frightened the soldiers. Those who served in that conflict certainly found them to be a compelling subject, but a historical filmmaker at the end of the twentieth century had a more secular approach to the experience of battle. He said,

> They're not out there supporting causes—freeing slaves or liberation or religion—but trying to keep themselves and their buddies alive. That's the most important thing on earth. Not freeing anyone, just staying alive. We invent a version of heaven and hell to superimpose upon the randomness of our existence, something formal and conclusive on something that is neither, and it's understandable why humans want to do that.[20]

Gardiner H. Shattuck Jr. made an extensive study of the revivals that broke out during the war, events in which the subject of eternity constantly arose and, he believes, made an indelible mark on the soldiers' lives. A "Great Revival" occurred in late 1863 in the Army of Northern Virginia and continued until May of the following year when an attack by General Grant broke it up. In that period, about seven thousand men, or 10 percent of Lee's army, came to faith in Christ. Similarly, lengthy prayer meetings characterized the lives of the soldiers who defended Georgia that winter, resulting in many conversions. In a dramatic story from that time, Private Sam Watkins of the 1st Tennessee Regiment spoke of ten soldiers who were kneeling at the "mourners' bench" when an old tree ignited from the sparks of the campfire. With great suddenness, it fell on the men and crushed them. In his account, Watkins expressed more gladness than remorse because "their souls had joined 'the army of the hosts of heaven.'"[21]

Shattuck writes that many Confederate commanders accepted Christ during that time, including General John Bell Hood, who'd been severely wounded on the battlefield. The Episcopal Bishop of Arkansas, Henry Lay, was present during the General's baptism in which Hood, "unable to kneel . . . supported himself on his crutch and staff, and with bowed head received the benediction."[22]

Somewhere between one hundred thousand and two hundred thousand Union soldiers made professions of faith during the war, while in the smaller Confederate forces, at least one hundred thousand did so. How many more, however, who were already believers did the revivals encourage and inspire?[23]

From his investigation into the lives of soldiers touched by Christ, Shattuck observed that having "a disciplined religious life . . . was considered useful for a soldier. Since the assurance of eternal salvation removed the fear of death, religious soldiers were presumed to exhibit more heroism than their unconverted comrades." Furthermore, he observed:

> The battlefield was "the valley of the shadow of death" to everyone who crossed it, but Christians felt they gained some mastery over its dangers by surrendering their claims to being in control. Stray bullets and cannonballs often struck down even the most wary, convincing pious men that God's inscrutable providence alone protected their bodies and souls. William Russell of the 26th Virginia Regiment recorded this prayer in his diary: "Oh Lord, if we should go into battle, be thou our shield & hiding place. If it is consistent with thy will, that any of us should be killed, may we have a happy admittance into thy Kingdom above."[24]

The Rev. William W. Bennett headed the Methodist Soldiers' Tract Association during the war. He also wrote one of the pamphlets, *A Narrative of the Great Revival Which Prevailed in the Southern Armies*, in which he referred to the Confederate camps as "a school of Christ." He noted that in General Lee's army at the Rappahonnock,

> The revival flame swept through every corps, division, brigade, and regiment. [One chaplain explained]: "The whole army is a vast field, ready and ripe to the harvest. . . . The susceptibility of the soldiery to the gospel is wonderful, and, doubtful as the remark may appear, the military camp is most favorable to the work of revival. The soldiers, with the simplicity of little children, listen to and embrace the truth."[25]

The tracts distributed to the soldiers addressed heaven and hell, pressing them to be quick about their decisions for or against Christ since they didn't know how long they had to live. The descriptions were often vivid, designed to elicit an emotional response. The Evangelical Tract Society of Petersburg, Virginia, which operated until the fall of the city in April 1865, published "Refuge from the Storm: There is a Storm to Which Man is Exposed." In it, the writer used the story of Noah as a backdrop to explain how urgent the hour was and how terrible the consequences of disbelief:

> The storm of forty days and forty nights which drowned the old world was long indeed, but it had an end; and in the dispersing clouds was seen the bow of promise that the earth should no more be destroyed by a flood. There have been long storms since, but none without an end. Some have been dreadful while they lasted; but their end, when the sun again appeared in the heavens, or the moon and the stars were seen, has filled the hearts of men with joy. But that storm to which the wicked are exposed, shall have no end. Its clouds shall never be dispersed; no bow of promise will ever appear to the tempest-driven souls who experience its merciless peltings; no sun to them will ever rise and shine; no moon, no stars appear. That storm will ever be gathering blackness; it will ever be increasing in fury.... To that night there will be no morning; to that storm there will be no termination.... Oh, whose heart does not melt within him at the thought of his exposure to such a doom? Yet this is just the exposure of every impenitent man![26]

Those who waited on the home front for loved ones to return also found solace in their faith that this world with its troubles would soon pass away. Their deepest yearnings were for the perfection of heaven, where they would be reunited with those who did not return. They didn't speak as Americans do today about the dead "looking down on them"; rather, those who remained looked up, to God and their eternal home.

On June 10, 1861, an anonymous mother wrote a letter to her daughter in which she spoke of the ability of a sustaining faith in Christ. Her attitude reflected the way that generation of Americans faced death, which was such a frequent visitor:

> *"My dear Daughter. . . . Death is solemn. To lay a beloved friend in the silent tomb is a heavy trial, but Oh! there are much heavier trials than Death. There is a sweet comfort to the heart when we have good hope our friend rests in the bosom of eternal life. But, oh it requires fortitude, strength and heroism to battle with living troubles."*[27]

THE CRITICAL
PERIOD

O
n the afternoon of April 9, 1865, General Robert E. Lee surrendered his starving army to Ulysses S. Grant at Appomattox Courthouse, Virginia. It was difficult to find families on either side of the conflict that had not been touched in some way by the Civil War's four years of wreckage. One Maine woman had watched her husband and five sons march off to war in 1861; her spouse was badly wounded within the first year and sent home. One son was hurt at Bull Run, and three of his brothers died at the Battle of Gettysburg. After the first son was reinjured, he received a discharge but was so weak that he froze to death on his way from the railroad station. Only one son survived the war but he, too, had been hurt badly.[1]

With the surrender, the fatigued nation breathed a collective sigh of relief, but less than a week later a new wave of grief flooded the country when President Abraham Lincoln was assassinated. As they draped their homes and businesses in black, they wondered, "How could this have happened on top of everything else we've lost?" Their collective belief that the President had gone to a just reward in heaven soothed the rawness of their emotions. In his eulogy, Henry Champion Deming told the General Assembly of Connecticut, "The nation stands aghast! The crime of the Dark Ages has entered our History—stealthy assassination has broken the sacred succession of the people's anointed—the life of the best beloved of Presidents is oozing from a murderous wound—the soul of Abraham Lincoln is transferred from Earth to Heaven."[2]

At the funeral in the White House, Dr. Phineas D. Gurley of the New York Avenue Presbyterian Church didn't speculate on Lincoln's eternal condition but focused on his sterling character. He assured the nation that God was still sovereign and could be trusted in spite of this latest tragedy:

> He is dead; but the God in whom he trusted lives, and He can guide and strengthen his successor, as He guided and strengthened him. He is dead; but the memory of his virtues, of his wise and patriotic counsels and labors, of his calm and steady faith in God lives, is precious, and will be a power for good in the country quite down to the end of time. He is dead; but the cause he so ardently loved, so ably, patiently, faithfully represented and defended—not for himself only, not for us only, but for all people in all their coming generations, till time shall be no more—that cause survives his fall, and will survive it.[3]

President Lincoln was shot on Good Friday, and on Easter Sunday throughout the newly restored nation other pastors spoke of him in their sermons, frequently casting him as a martyr and a latter-day Moses. In New York, the Rev. Dr. N. L. Rice constantly reassured his congregation that in spite of such a terrible thing happening in a Christian nation, they could, according to Psalm 46, be still and know that God was still God.[4] Like other ministers, he spoke of Lincoln's many glowing qualities and praised him as a good man who steered the "ship of state" through the Civil War. Even in that sentimental era, they didn't say he was "up there looking down on us." Rather, most people believed that as a God-fearing man, Lincoln had gone to his rest and that those left behind should try to emulate his Christian character and get close enough to God that they also would go to heaven when they died. In a Lincoln funeral sermon in Philadelphia, the Rev. Phillips Brooks preached along those lines, in order "to remind his audience of the greatness of Lincoln's life, to help them be aware of those causes that culminated in the president's death, and a challenge to be worthy of that life that had been lived among them."[5]

Brooks ended with the appeal, "May God make us worthy of the memory of Abraham Lincoln!"[6] This was the sort of message that most of that period's ministers gave when a devout person died.

As Lincoln's funeral train made its way to the President's burial in Illinois, emotional crowds paid their last respects at each stop. Few among them would have thought the great leader could now be anywhere but in heaven. H. H. Cody captured the national mood in his song "The Death Knell Is Tolling." It carries with it a sense that as citizens of a Christian nation, Americans were grieving hard, but not as those who had no hope:

> The death knell is tolling, the flag at half-mast,
> The land drap'd in mourning, we all stand aghast,
> As the tidings so fearful are borne to our ears;
> And today we are bending in sorrow and tears
> O'er a President's grave, 'round a newly wrought tomb,
> Made by deeds of such darkness that horror and gloom,
> Spread a pall o'er the land while a great nation weeps,
> O'er the form of the dead who so peacefully sleeps.
>
> Yes, peacefully sleeps, heeding not the foul hand
> That is stain'd with the choicest life-blood of the land,
> Heeding not the wild waves of anguish that roll
> O'er the hearts of all true men, chilling the soul,
> His mission accomplish'd, his life work is o'er,
> The tumults of earth shall disturb him no more;
> Great Martyr of Freedom! he has gone to his God,
> And we're left to weep, and "Pass under the rod."
>
> O God of our Fathers! we look up to thee;
> In this hour of sadness, here bending the knee;
> We crave thy protection in the midst of the gloom,
> As we stand the third time, by a President's tomb;
> Our way lies in darkness, and the old ship of State
> Droops colors in mourning, o'er her Captain's sad fate;
> But with Thee at the helm, our flag shall still wave
> "O'er the land of the free, and the home of the brave."
> Sleep, sleep, sleep, Lincoln sleep, sleep.[7]

❦

While Northerners were bowed down by President Lincoln's death, Southerners reeled in the days after their surrender and the assassination. The President's killer was from Maryland, and their homes, farms, businesses, and public places were shells of their former proud selves. Cities and rural areas alike had experienced such devastation that there wasn't enough money for the most basic civil services; virtually no banks operated, and the transportation system and infrastructure were reduced to rubble. The railroads were not completely restored for at least two decades. There was widespread starvation. Georgia poet Sydney Lanier remarked, "Pretty much the whole of life has been merely not dying."[8] In the most precarious situation of all were the former slaves, newly emancipated but with their champion in the grave. Of them Frederick Douglass said, "He was free from the old quarter that once gave him shelter, but a slave to the rains of summer and the frosts of winter."[9]

The federal government undertook a program of Southern reconstruction that lasted until 1877, but even then the South remained in an educationally, socially, and technologically backward state for some time. Although Northern families had also endured terrible losses, they were in a far better position, at least economically.

In the aftermath of the tremendous destruction and loss of life, there was a surge of interest in spiritualism, the practice of trying to conjure dead spirits, but most Americans chose to let traditional Christian faith guide them through the challenges. Between 1860 and 1870, church membership and attendance flourished. The Methodists and Baptists saw increases of 22 percent, the Presbyterians improved their numbers by 24 percent, and the Episcopalians advanced by 46 percent. "Here was a 'church-going' America on an unprecedented scale," says Martin Marty.[10] Some ministers became national celebrities, "princes of the pulpit," whose opinions were widely quoted in the papers—men like Henry Ward Beecher, Phillips Brooks, Russell Conwell, Dwight L. Moody, and

Charles Hodge, along with the female evangelist Phoebe Palmer. Beecher, Brooks, and Conwell in particular, who led large urban churches, gave "public shape to a Protestant culture."[11] Beecher, the most famous minister in the immediate postwar period, wasn't loathe to point out that the North was ready to lead the charge into a new American era. He proclaimed, "We are to have charge of this continent. [The South] has been proved, and has been found wanting. She is not worthy to bear rule. . . . This continent is to be from this time forth governed by Northern men, with Northern ideas, and with a Northern gospel. . . . The North has been true to the cause of Christ."[12]

Beecher and Brooks took it upon themselves to mediate Christianity to the modern world that was challenging it in several ways.[13] The Civil War had divided many denominations; the rise of the urban industrial state and shifting immigration patterns were challenging establishment Protestantism. In addition, the arrival of historical criticism of the Bible that had first begun in European academies was making an appearance among some American colleges and universities. This method of interpretation regarded the Bible as any other historical document, and it emerged around the same time as Darwin's theory of evolution. Arthur Meier Schlesinger has called this era "the critical period in American religion."[14]

∽◦∾

Beecher, Brooks, and Conwell, along with others of their more theologically liberal manner, were not the only public Christian figures during this period. Others were shaping the way in which Americans framed their beliefs about sin and salvation, heaven and hell. Among them was the most prominent evangelical of the postwar era, Dwight L. Moody. Born in Massachusetts, Moody had a hard childhood that included his alcoholic father's death when he was four. At eighteen, he became a Christian while working in his uncle's shoe store, then he moved to Chicago a year later where he began a long and illustrious ministry. He eventually created the largest Sunday school of his time with an average attendance of 650. After the war he teamed up with singer/ songwriter Ira Sankey to present evangelistic crusades first in England, then to enormous crowds throughout America. Together they created a prototype that other evangelists followed for generations, including Billy Graham. Moody's overriding concern was saving souls. He said, "I look upon this world as a wrecked vessel. God has given me a lifeboat and said to me, 'Moody, save all you can.'"[15] His background and delivery weren't polished like Beecher's or Brooks's, but he was just as influential in his day, and newspapers frequently published his sermons, many of which were put into book form.

Once he was traveling by train when he saw a boy selling books by the popular orator Robert Ingersoll. The former Civil War colonel was causing a national sensation by openly professing agnosticism and generally disparaging anything Christian. His books sold well, and his public appearances were widely attended, largely because people were curious about him. The newsboy on the train kept calling out, "Ingersoll on Hell! Ingersoll on Hell!" Moody put a copy of his own book in the boy's other hand, and the fellow continued on his way shouting, "Ingersoll on Hell, Moody on Heaven!"[16] When Ingersoll died some years later, Moody spoke of him, respectfully, as a lost soul:

> My feeling toward him, has always been that of deepest pity, for a life
> like his seems so barren of everything that has made my life joyous
> and blessed. How dark must be the life of a man for whom, by his own
> confession, it was like "a narrow vale between the peaks of two eternities;
> we cry aloud and the only answer is the echo of our calling," and for
> whom death seemed like "a leap into the dark." How different from that
> of a believer in Christ! For him not only is the present life filled with the
> peace of God, but the future is bright with hope. He knows that for him
> death is only the exchanging of a shifting tent for an enduring mansion.[17]

When an interviewer asked Moody if he thought Ingersoll had died without any hope of heaven, the evangelist said, "I don't know. I don't see how a man can live without such a hope. It must be terrible. We are not his judges. It is for God alone to judge him."[18]

Some critics accused Moody of being unorthodox because he didn't preach about hell as much as earlier revivalists. Although he firmly believed that judgment followed death and would result in hell for many, Moody said that he disliked preaching about it.[19] Stanley N. Gundry observes that Moody believed "the existence of hell and the futility of the efforts of the unconverted to escape were an integral part of the rationale behind all of [his] preaching. . . . His sermons contain frequent incidental references to hell, the wrath of God, and future judgment."[20] In one sermon, Moody talked about why he didn't often mention hell:

> A man came to me the other day and said: "I like your preaching. You don't preach hell, and I suppose you don't believe in one." Now I don't want any one to rise up in the Judgment and say that I was not a faithful preacher of the Word of God. It is my duty to preach God's Word just as He gives it to me; I have no right to pick a text here and there, and say, "I don't believe that." If I throw out one text I must throw out all, for in the same Bible I read of rewards and punishments, Heaven and hell.
>
> No one ever drew such a picture of hell as the Son of God. No one could do it, for He alone knew what the future would be. He didn't keep back this doctrine of retribution, but preached it out plainly; preached it, too, with pure love, just as a mother would warn her son of the end of his course of sin.[21]

There were many other biblically orthodox leaders of that era who continued to believe in established Christian teachings about the afterlife, especially heaven for the saved and hell for the damned. Among them was evangelist and author Phoebe Palmer. In a poem she addressed the problem of alcohol, which was pictured as an adder about to steal a man's soul and consign it to hell:

> What did *nerve* to that hand impart
> Which took a fellow's life?
> It was that ADDER he drank up!
> It was that poisonous sting

He swallowed from *that* whiskey-cup!
That *living* venomed thing
Still gathers strength from every sip,
Frenzies his fevered frame!
Oft as he puts it to his lip
He feeds anew the flame!
And soon the awful fires of hell
Will seize upon his SOUL!
And heaven's eternal records tell
The *whole, the fearful* WHOLE![22]

Frances Willard, who led the Women's Christian Temperance Union, also believed in the link between alcoholism and damnation. The most admired and photographed female of her time, Willard had two great passions, her love for Jesus Christ and ridding the country of alcohol. She was known to instill the fear of God's wrath whenever she challenged saloon operators. During one of her "Woman's Crusade" campaigns, she and a few dozen followers stood outside a Chicago bar in subfreezing temperatures singing, praying, and chanting the 146th Psalm. They had already managed to close fifteen saloons in a week's time, charging that people who ran such establishments not only were responsible for the ruination of many a man and his family, but were going to be eternally damned if they failed to repent. When the owner came out and began cursing the women, Willard just prayed louder:

O God, in the name of our desolate homes, blasted hopes, ruined lives, for the honor of our community, for our happiness, for the good name of our town, in the name of Jesus Christ sweating out the passion of the cross, for the sake of this soul which will be lost, make this man cleanse himself from his heinous sin. O God, open his ears that we may beg, may implore him. . . .

The bartender clapped his hands to his head and uttered a howl, "Stop it! Stop it! You can have the place, but I won't have you praying my soul into hell!"[23]

༄༅༄

The prevailing beliefs of that time about heaven and hell continued to be in a traditional and orthodox vein. While some in higher education were beginning to question those concepts, it is worthwhile to note that colleges were moving away from exclusively training clergy in favor of raising up men to be industrial and scientific leaders. College also became a place for young men to build up their social resumes. A spirit of skepticism that emerged from Europe had not yet filtered very far down to the average Protestant pulpit or pew. From his distinguished position at Princeton Seminary, theologian Charles Hodge still taught that "God and Christ, holiness and sin, heaven and hell, really are what the Bible declares them to be."[24] Edward McKinley maintains,

> The great majority of professing Christians had strictly orthodox beliefs, and regarded Darwin or Higher Criticism, to the extent that they thought about them at all, as annoying European nonsense, just the sort of thing that proved the superiority of American thinking on such things. . . . But certainly by the late 19th century some intellectuals and theologians were troubled, and evolutionary thinking and Higher Criticism, which became influential among elite thinkers who thought of themselves as part of a larger Atlantic cultural community, became a factor in these circles. To counter this, many famous preachers took a strong stand, and that position was much more important among ordinary believers.[25]

The Salvation Army, a British organization that was developing in the United States at that time, often referred to heaven and hell in its meetings. McKinley says,

> The Army ministers (officers) believed in the literal reality of Heaven and Hell and preached these things very often. A lot of the old Salvation Army songs—both those written by the Army people themselves, and those shared with the other Protestant churches, were unashamed in proclaiming the joys of Heaven for the saved, and the terrors of Hell for those who rejected Christ or backslid.[26]

In one of General William Booth's most famous sermons, he portrayed a Christian standing on the edge of eternity "watching in horror as thousands of souls poured over the edge into Hell—Booth urged the believers to act, to reach out, to save as many as could be saved by any means, because nothing else could matter as much."[27]

In that era, Christians were also painting an increasingly emotional picture of heaven. Sydney Ahlstrom refers to it as "the most extravagantly sentimental period in (American) history," and holds that it was teams of revivalists like those led by Moody who perpetuated that condition through "song and sermon."[28] In popular hymns of that day, heaven was often portrayed as a great resting place for the souls of the redeemed in Jesus. Among them was "We'll Never Say Goodbye," written in 1894 by the prolific Fanny Crosby and composed by Ira Sankey:

O blessed home where those who meet
Shall never say goodbye;
Where kindred souls each other greet,
And never say goodbye.

Refrain

We'll never say goodbye,
We'll never say goodbye;
In that fair land beyond the sky,
We'll never say goodbye.

Beyond this vale of toil and care,
We'll never say goodbye;
We part in tears on earth, but there—
We'll never say goodbye

Refrain

When safe among the ransomed throng
We'll never say goodbye;
Where life is one eternal song,
We'll never say goodbye.

Refrain

On yonder fair and peaceful shore,
We'll never say goodbye;
But dwell with Christ forevermore,
And never say goodbye.

Earlier, Crosby had written "Safe in the Arms of Jesus" (1868), another sentimental hymn about death and heaven that enjoyed great popularity after being performed at President Grant's funeral in 1885:

Safe in the arms of Jesus, safe on His gentle breast,
There by His love o'ershaded, sweetly my soul shall rest.
Hark! 'tis the voice of angels, borne in a song to me.
Over the fields of glory, over the jasper sea.

Refrain

Safe in the arms of Jesus, safe on His gentle breast
There by His love o'ershaded, sweetly my soul shall rest.

Safe in the arms of Jesus, safe from corroding care,
Safe from the world's temptations, sin cannot harm me there.
Free from the blight of sorrow, free from my doubts and fears;
Only a few more trials, only a few more tears!

Refrain

Jesus, my heart's dear Refuge, Jesus has died for me;
Firm on the Rock of Ages, ever my trust shall be.
Here let me wait with patience, wait till the night is over;
Wait till I see the morning break on the golden shore.

Protestant preachers in the late nineteenth century often used the image of the church as a lifeboat in an ocean of floundering lost souls with the members in the lifeboat holding out their hands and ropes to save the lost. Otherwise they would sink forever without their help.[29] Those who navigated the waters with Jesus as their captain would make their final voyage "across Jordan" to the "Promised Land" of heaven.

A FUTURE, BUT WHAT KIND
OF HOPE?

A year before the illustrious American author Mark Twain died, he published his last book, an irreverent description of sea captain Elias Stormfield's long and circuitous trip to paradise. In *Captain Stormfield's Visit to Heaven*, Twain portrayed the crusty old salt hurtling round outer space on a comet for thirty years, uncertain about where he'd end up, before he at last arrived at the pearly gates. To his great disappointment, heaven wasn't quite what Stormfield expected, as he related to his friend, Peters:

> When I found myself perched on a cloud, with a million other people, I never felt so good in my life. Says I, "Now this is according to the promises; I've been having my doubts, but now I am in heaven, sure enough." I gave my palm branch a wave or two, for luck, and then I tautened up my harp-strings and struck in. Well, Peters, you can't imagine anything like the row we made. It was grand to listen to, and made a body thrill all over, but there was considerable many tunes going on at once, and that was a drawback to the harmony, you understand; and then there was a lot of Injun tribes, and they kept up such another war-whooping that they kind of took the tuck out of the music. By and by I quit performing, and judged I'd take a rest.
>
> There was quite a nice mild old gentleman sitting next me, and I noticed he didn't take a hand; I encouraged him, but he said he was naturally bashful, and was afraid to try before so many people. By and by the old gentleman said he never could seem to enjoy music somehow. The fact

was, I was beginning to feel the same way; but I didn't say anything. Him and I had a considerable long silence, then, but of course it warn't noticeable in that place. After about sixteen or seventeen hours, during which I played and sung a little, now and then—always the same tune, because I didn't know any other—I laid down my harp and begun to fan myself with my palm branch. Then we both got to sighing pretty regular. Finally, says he—"Don't you know any tune but the one you've been pegging at all day?"

"Not another blessed one," says I.

"Don't you reckon you could learn another one?" says he.

"Never," says I; "I've tried to, but I couldn't manage it."

"It's a long time to hang to the one—eternity, you know."

"Don't break my heart," says I; "I'm getting low-spirited enough already."

After another long silence, says he—"Are you glad to be here?"

Says I, "Old man, I'll be frank with you. This AIN'T just as near my idea of bliss as I thought it was going to be, when I used to go to church."[1]

A year after the book came out, Twain himself had to face the same death he'd written so flippantly about, and in the popular press of the time, few speculated about the journey that his soul had embarked upon, which was usually the case with prominent people. Although he wasn't always or consistently antagonistic toward the Christian faith, he did tend to treat it lightly and at times nurtured negative thoughts about it, especially during dark periods of loss. After all, one of his famous quotes was "Faith is believing something you know ain't true." At one time he wrote some especially scathing things that might have incited the public had they been printed while he was alive, "anti-religious essays that were so shocking his own daughter Clara kept them secret for almost 30 years."[2] He'd written them after the deaths of his wife and another daughter, during a time of personal and financial depression. In the compositions he referred to humans as "long-suffering victims deluded by their own ludicrous religious beliefs."[3]

Since no one could write with any degree of veracity that the beloved author had gone to heaven, which was a popular component of obituaries and eulogies, most public utterances were of a more general nature. President McKinley simply lauded him as defining the American literary tradition, a man who had written wholesome stories that families could comfortably read together. Twain's literary friend, Dr. Henry van Dyke, author of *The Other Wise Man*, gave the funeral message in which he praised the author's best attributes and said he hoped that Twain would have the rest of an honorable person.

It's highly unlikely that an American publisher would have printed his glib story of the afterlife a generation earlier; in fact, Twain actually wrote *Captain Stormfield* forty years before its release. At the opening of the twentieth century, however, while the United States was still overwhelmingly informed by Protestant mores and leadership, the culture was not as orthodox, or homogeneous, as it had been one hundred, or even fifty years earlier. From the period right before the Civil War until 1921, over twenty-five million immigrants arrived. Initially, most of the newcomers hailed from Northern and Western Europe and were largely mainstream Christian in their beliefs and customs. They did come from a variety of denominations, however. By the turn of the century, most immigrants were arriving from Central, Eastern, and Southern Europe, mostly non-Protestant areas.[4] Catholics and Jews made up the majority of those numbers. There were stark religious differences between them and native-born Americans, many of whom considered Catholics to be sinister subordinates of the pope. Some even considered the pontiff to be the Antichrist. Catholic immigrants brought with them long-established attitudes about heaven and hell that often were filled with medieval imagery and anxiety about mortal and venial sins.

Jewish beliefs, on the other hand, were a mixed bag, depending upon where the person came from and what branch of Judaism they practiced.

According to historian Robert Weiner, "Almost all traditionally orthodox Jews, which means about half of the immigrants from eastern Europe, still had a vague belief in heaven, in God's ultimate reward and justice for those who lived just lives."[5] Those from the European countries most affected by the eighteenth-century Enlightenment had less of a longing for the afterlife and definitely did not think of it along the dramatic delineations of the Protestants.

There were also other immigrants, non-European ones, who brought with them more exotic views about the afterlife. Among them were the Chinese, who arrived on the West Coast for the primary purpose of building the railroads. According to Ting Ting Yan Davis, one of China's top novelists and screenwriters in the pre-Tiananmen Square era:

> Those who believed in Buddha thought there would be a hell and reincarnation. If you are a good person and do things right in this lifetime, your next life will be good or better. Otherwise you go to hell, get tortured there, and you never come back, or have a lot of suffering in your next life. Maybe you can't be a person but a horse or cow and will have to do unbearable labor for men. When Confucius was asked about death, his answer was, "Not knowing life, how could you know death?" His teachings were about standards of good living but were not a religion. This was what most Chinese common people believed in 1900. The Chinese didn't think much about an afterlife.[6]

In spite of the perceived strangeness of their beliefs and customs, immigrants had a profound impact on the culture even as they were being Americanized. At the Ford Motor Company, for example, they could go to school to learn English and rules of good citizenship. At the graduation ceremony, they did a play in which they dressed in their national costumes and climbed into an enormous melting pot.

When they climbed back out, all of them were wearing "American" outfits and waving the stars and stripes.[7] Even so, as they lived and worked among Americans, immigrants brought their own beliefs and traditions to bear upon their new home. They established new churches and put their own stamp on the neighborhoods in which they lived. They became nannies and housekeepers, sharing their customs with their employers. In Texas, Arizona, California, and New Mexico, the population of Mexicans skyrocketed between 1900 and 1910, and they completely altered that region.[8] In addition, while immigrants learned the fundamentals of American Protestantism as the "norm," that standard was itself changing.

∽∘∾

On October 11, 1844, a misguided group of Christians dressed in white robes and climbed to the highest point of buildings, houses, and haystacks to await Christ's second coming and their glorious ascent into heaven. They had quit their jobs and sold homes and businesses at the encouragement of their spiritual leader, a farmer-turned-pastor named William Miller. He believed that according to certain "day-year" calculations of biblical prophecies, he could tell approximately when Christ would return to earth. Some of his zealous supporters thought they could determine the exact time and arrived at October 11, 1844. They were sorely disappointed, as well as discredited, when the sun also rose on October 12, but their *premillenial* proclivities remained a strong force in some Protestant circles for the rest of the century, and into the new one.

By 1900, however, they faced stiff competition from a different group, the *postmillennialists*, who believed that specific prophecies from the book of Revelation were playing out in current events. In Revelation 20, there is a reference to the thousand-year reign of Christ, or the millennium, and postmillennialists believed that would be the last era of world history. "During this time," explains George Marsden, "the Holy Spirit would be poured out and the Gospel spread around the world, Christ would return after this millennial age (hence 'postmillennialism') and would bring history to an end." Postmillennialists were on the whole optimistic about societal progress in spiritual matters. "They saw human history as reflecting an ongoing struggle between cosmic forces of God and Satan, each well represented by various earthly powers, but with the victory of righteousness ensured."[9]

Both types of millennialists agreed that theirs was a cosmic battle between good and evil, Christ and Satan, for the souls of humans. They also concurred that some prophetic Bible passages could be understood literally and were being fulfilled in certain events of their time. What they mainly disagreed about was whether or not Christ would return before the millennium, His thousand-year golden reign of the church on earth. Premillennialists had a less upbeat view of progress, and they interpreted Scripture in a much more literal manner than their counterparts.[10]

Postmillennialists were friends of modern progress who expected even greater technological and human advances in the coming years. Social advancement was a primary goal of theirs, and they didn't concern themselves with prophetic timelines or the more dramatic aspects of the coming kingdom of God. James Moorehead says, "They stopped depicting hell in lurid detail . . . stressed the natural over the supernatural, and generally emphasized this life over the life to come."[11] Eschewing white robes and haystacks, these Protestants sought to bring God's kingdom to earth through foreign missions, church federations, and something called the Social Gospel.

The struggle for the kingdom wasn't just between believers and nonbelievers anymore. As in many other times throughout church history, the conflicts were internal as well.

∽o∾

There had always been disputes and differences between various denominations about methods of worship, which doctrines were the most important, and how to live out the teachings of Jesus Christ in everyday life. In those debates, however, most American Protestants had at least agreed on the starting points or the essential beliefs of faith and practice. These included the virgin birth of Christ, the exclusivity of salvation through faith in Christ alone, the doctrine of the Trinity, the authority and reliability of Scripture, and the return of Christ. At this time, however, a small number of ministers, along with some college and seminary professors, were being influenced by European ideas and calling into question fundamental aspects of Christian faith and practice. These men were led increasingly by the scientific and modern spirit of the times. They emphasized progress through reason and disdained anything suggesting the supernatural—there could be no allowances for miracles or revelation. Protestant leaders manned their posts, armed for battle with their particular interpretations of the Bible and the creeds, while the laity, still standing mainly on conservative ground, watched and tried to make sense of it all.

On the side of Christian orthodoxy and tradition, those from the revivalist and Calvinist camps continued to make a significant contribution to American life and thought. D. L. Moody had died in 1899, but others continued to conduct evangelistic campaigns including R. A. Torry and the memorable Billy Sunday. In the 1880s, Sunday had been a popular baseball player with the Chicago White Stockings, an outfielder whose exuberant base running and fielding delighted fans. He gave up his athletic career after being converted to faith in Jesus Christ, and he began preaching in Midwestern churches where he honed his gifts for plain speaking and theatrics rivaling those of George Whitefield. He declined several lucrative offers to return to baseball, including contracts anywhere from $400 to $2,000 per month, when the average American worker made $480 a year.[12]

The Iowa-born Sunday became America's best-known revivalist in the opening decades of the twentieth century, a preacher who encouraged people to "walk the sawdust trail" to Christ and away from sin and hell. His beliefs went along the lines of mainstream, evangelical Protestantism—the authority and inerrancy of Scripture, the virgin birth, the substitutionary atonement of Christ, His bodily resurrection, the reality of Satan and hell, and Jesus' imminent second coming. Although Sunday was well read, he wasn't a scholar by any means. At his ordination examination to become a Presbyterian minister in 1903, he answered "That's too deep for me," or "I'll have to pass that up" when the questions about history and theology became too involved. He once said, "I don't know any more about theology than a jack-rabbit knows about ping pong, but I'm on my way to glory."[13] His approach to matters of heaven and hell was no-holds-barred; there was no halfway. A person was headed to one place or the other.

Far less flamboyant than Billy Sunday, B. B. Warfield also held firmly to orthodoxy from his position of leadership at Princeton Theological Seminary. Although both were Presbyterians, unlike Sunday, Warfield was no fan of revivalism, believing that the movement lent itself to subjective religious experiences instead of a deep and abiding faith. He believed that the best expression of Christian faith could be found in the teachings of John Calvin and the Westminster Confession of Faith. Warfield said that Modernism could never supercede those teachings, although he was not entirely opposed to Darwinism. He thought that if one clearly understood that God alone guided the process of evolution, then there didn't have to be a divorce between science and Christianity on that subject.

Other leaders in American Protestantism at that time approached the Christian faith far differently. Known as theological "liberals," these thinkers were chiefly Arminian—they viewed humans as free agents who could choose on their own whether or not to accept God's offer of salvation. Unlike their conservative counterparts, however, liberals tended to believe that there was no original sin or natural depravity in the first place, but that people have a natural ability for unselfishness. The main reason that people sin is because of such factors as a lack of education or privilege. Therefore, if people had the moral example of Jesus to follow, as well as ample opportunities for education and personal advancement, there would be no more sin.[14]

There were two kinds of liberals at the turn of the century, the evangelical liberals and the modernist liberals. The latter group was much smaller and more radical, believing that religion was a human invention, and the Bible a great book among many others like it. In such a system there was little room for heaven and hell, nor was there any need, they said, to promote Christianity as being superior to other religions. This view's chief spokesmen were William James and Josiah Royce. In his 1890 book *The Principles of Psychology*, James wrote, "The hell to be endured hereafter, of which theology tells, is no worse than the hell we make for ourselves in this world by habitually fashioning our characters in the wrong way."[15]

Yet, it was the other set of liberals, the so-called "evangelical" ones, who had the most influence on American thought in their day, mostly because they spoke in a nonthreatening, more palatable way than the more strident and iconoclastic modernist liberals.[16] These thinkers upheld the historic doctrines and traditions, as well as the importance of the Bible, but they believed that adjustments needed to be made to accommodate the modern world with its advances in the hard and social sciences, technology, and education.[17] This approach to theology had its biggest impact in the Northeast, in the Congregational, Methodist, Episcopal, Disciples of Christ, Presbyterian, and Northern Baptist Convention churches. Least impacted were the Roman Catholics and Lutherans, as well as more conservative evangelical groups in both urban and rural areas.[18]

The chief spokesman for evangelical liberalism was the Baptist pastor Walter Rauschenbusch, the son of a theologically orthodox German pastor who taught at Rochester Theological Seminary. Rauschenbusch's own view of Christianity began to diverge from the teachings of his youth when he encountered the challenges of European-style higher criticism. He came to believe that the kingdom of God was not so much about saving people's souls so they could go to heaven as it was a matter of "transforming the life on earth into the harmony of heaven."[19] He held that Jesus did not die for the sins of the world in a substitutionary atonement, but that He died instead "to substitute love for selfishness as the basis of human society." An essential element of the liberalism he championed came to be known as the "Social Gospel." Christians from earlier eras had made

substantial inroads and efforts at societal reform, but this was differ-
ent. Its goal was to transform society, not to save individual souls, which
Rauschenbusch considered the height of human selfishness. In his book
A Theology for the Social Gospel, Rauschenbusch said:

> Other things being equal, a solidaristic religious experience is more
> distinctively Christian than an individualistic religious experience. To be
> afraid of hell or purgatory and desirous of a life without pain or trouble
> in heaven was not in itself Christian. It was self-interest on a higher
> level. It is not strange that men were wholly intent on saving themselves
> as long as such dangers as Dante describes were real to their minds. A
> man might be pardoned for forgetting his entire social consciousness
> if he found himself dangling over a blazing pit. But even in more
> spiritual forms of conversion, as long as men are wholly intent on their
> own destiny, they do not necessarily emerge from selfishness. It only
> changes its form. A Christian regeneration must have an outlook toward
> humanity and result in a higher social consciousness.[20]

Rauschenbusch also took Jonathan Edwards's teachings about heaven
and hell to task, making a total break with America's Calvinist roots, as
well as centuries-old thought, which he deemed "unethical." Past believers had not focused on living a righteous life oriented toward society, he
charged. If contemporary Christians continued to think along those lines,
he said, they would be going against the very ways of God, ways which had
been misunderstood in times past when people had been understandably
ignorant, but for which there was no longer an excuse:

> If we learned in heaven that a minority were in hell, we should look at
> God to see what he was going to do about it; and if he did nothing, we
> should look at Jesus to see how this harmonized with what he taught
> us about his Father; and if he did nothing, something would die out of
> heaven. Jonathan Edwards demanded that we should rejoice in the
> damnation of those whom the sovereign election of God abandoned
> to everlasting torment. Very justly, for we ought to be able to rejoice in
> what God does. But we can not rejoice in hell. It can't be done. At least
> by Christians. The more Christian Christ has made a soul, the more it

would mourn for the lost brothers. The conception of a permanent hell was tolerable only while God was conceived as an autocratic sovereign dealing with his subjects; it becomes intolerable when the Father deals with his children.[21]

Rauschenbusch desired that Christians live in such a way as to give society a massive makeover to usher in the kingdom of God on earth. Says Joseph Loconte, "As such, Rauschenbusch's gospel had little need of a Savior. It merely displaced the problem of evil—the supreme tragedy of the human soul in rebellion against God—with the challenge of social iniquities. The Kingdom of Heaven would come soon enough, if only we put our hands to the plow."[22]

Another leading liberal pastor in the early 1900s was Russell T. Conwell of Philadelphia. In an often-quoted sermon he told the story of a little girl who had given her "widow's mite" so that a new Sunday school could be built to accommodate the children who were turned away because there was no room. The girl became ill and died, but her righteous example motivated many others to give toward a new facility, which was constructed. Conwell said that while she had gone on to that "Shining World," she "still spoke" to believers about the value of giving from a sincere and pure heart. He imagined that from "the land on high," she was fellowshiping with the New Testament boy who gave the five loaves and two fishes to Jesus. Together they rejoiced that they had taught a great lesson in bringing about God's kingdom on earth. In the sermon Conwell made an allusion to the now-popular phrase that Americans so often use about the afterlife, one that he did not corroborate with Scripture:

Hattie May Wiatt looks down from the towers of Heaven upon this world and sees all these myriads of powerful influences moving out upon the earth and shaping the course of the world beyond anything we can dream. She is happy on high with the thought that her life was so full, that it was so complete, that she lived really to be so old in the influences she threw upon this earth.[23]

Russell Conwell was a theological liberal and an optimist, but unlike Rauschenbusch, he encouraged Christians to live to the best of their potential to advance themselves and not just God's kingdom. He thought that by pulling oneself up by the bootstraps, a person could become wealthy and that abundance was a sign of God's approval. He once said, "I say that you ought to get rich, and it is your duty to get rich."[24]

Another inspirational preacher of that era who fell under the rubric of the liberal evangelicals was Charles Sheldon, whose 1896 book became one of the first American "blockbusters." In fact, today's Christians still carry the book's theme around on bracelets and Bible covers—WWJD— "What would Jesus do?" *In His Steps* told the story of a complacent Midwestern congregation that was changed when a stranger came and challenged them to live according to the tenets of their faith. After the man died, the church's members took up his cry only to find that the kingdom of God had come to their town.

∽o∾

The theological liberals who ushered in the twentieth century largely anticipated a golden era, free of the embarrassing theatrics of revivalists and the beliefs of unsophisticated "hayseeds" who didn't know any better than to believe in virgin births, Jonah and the whale, individual salvation, and a literal heaven and hell. They believed that if they could just get people to abandon such superstitious nonsense and embrace scientific and modern social principles, while living out the Golden Rule, there would be no more poverty or disease, hunger or ignorance, violence or war. People's needs would then be met, and they would live harmoniously with others. They believed the country, indeed all of humanity, was standing on the brink of a new epoch, a "Christian Century," when the old would pass, and the new era of God's kingdom on earth would arrive. Martin Marty observed, "The social Christians were vulnerable theologically, as innovators often are. . . . The tragic dimensions of human existence were neglected in favor of the pervasive progressivism of the era."[25] No one could have foreseen just how tragic those human dimensions were, or how even the greatest technological advances could not save mankind from itself.

II

"CRACKS IN THE DIKE"

L ong ago and far away at a Methodist camp meeting, a ten-year-old Ohio boy went forward at the invitation and made a profession of faith in Jesus Christ. Afterward he said that his greatest ambition in life was to be "a true, earnest, and consistent Christian." Along the way, he also achieved one of the supreme honors this world can give, the presidency of the United States. At his March 4, 1897, inauguration, William McKinley told his audience:

> I assume the arduous and responsible duties of President of the United
> States, relying upon the support of my countrymen and invoking the
> guidance of Almighty God. Our faith teaches that there is no safer
> reliance than upon the God of our fathers, who has so singularly favored
> the American people in every national trial, and who will not forsake
> us so long as we obey His commandments and walk humbly in His
> footsteps.[1]

Among his core beliefs was that the American government bore a responsibility to spread both Western civilization and Christianity to the rest of the world. This conviction helped him determine that the United States should declare war against Spain in 1898, and when he appeared before Congress for that purpose, he said it was his hope that "our aspirations as a Christian, peace-loving people will be realized."[2] Most Americans agreed with their president that Spanish rule over Cuba and the Philippines needed to end. The *California Christian Advocate* proclaimed, "This war is the *Kingdom of God coming!*" Similarly, *The Nation* declared, "Coming to poor Cuba—the sunrise of a better day for the Philippines! . . . Oppression, cruelty, bigotry, superstition, and ignorance must down, and give a Christian civilization the right of way." "The cross will follow the flag," declared the *Pacific Advocate.* "The clock of the ages is striking."[3]

The United States won the brief war. Its foremost hero was a devout Christian and brash New Yorker named Theodore Roosevelt, who led a charge up San Juan Hill and went on to become McKinley's vice-president in the election of 1900. McKinley told an audience of his fellow Methodists what the war had meant to him:

> I am not ashamed to tell you, gentlemen, that I went down on my knees and prayed Almighty God for light and guidance more than one night. And one night late it came to me this way. . . . There was nothing left for us to do but to take them all and to educate the Filipinos and uplift and civilize and Christianize them and by God's grace do the very best we could by them, as our fellow men for whom Christ also died.[4]

After the Spanish-American War, as the sands of the nineteenth century ran out, the president felt confident about America's prospects for the new epoch. "At the outgoing of the old and the incoming of the new century," he said, "American liberty is more firmly established than ever before."[5] It seemed that nothing was to be impossible for the new nation in the new century. Of all the believers in the progress to come, none seemed more confident than theological liberals; yet it didn't take long after January 1, 1900, for their hopes to suffer multiple setbacks.

∽o∽

On September 5, 1901, President McKinley stood at the Pan American Exposition in Buffalo, New York, greeting well-wishers, when a young man named Leon Czolgosz ("Chol-gosh") approached him. Wielding a pistol that he'd concealed under a handkerchief, he fired twice. The first bullet nicked the President's shoulder, but the second one penetrated his stomach, colon, and kidneys. Czolgosz was a disgruntled anarchist, part of a popular movement well known in Europe that had its own vision for the new century. They devoted themselves to doing away with government and what they believed were elitist leaders in order to establish a new, more equitable order of society. In Europe, anarchists had assassinated Empress Elizabeth of Austria (1898) and King Humbert of Italy (1900), and had made an attempt on the life of the Prince of Wales that same year.

In the midst of the crisis in Buffalo, President McKinley kept his Christian composure, urging his protectors not to hurt his assailant and reciting the Lord's Prayer as he went under anesthesia for emergency surgery. At first it seemed that he would fully recover, and the tense nation breathed a little easier as its people waited and prayed, but several days later McKinley's health began to fail as gangrene swept through his body. He was to become the first American leader to be assassinated in the twentieth century.

While the president lay on his deathbed, his wife came to him, and he spoke tenderly, reassuringly to her about their mutual love for God. "God's will, not ours, be done," he whispered. "For his sake. For his sake," she whispered back to him, taking his hands and smiling at him through her tears. Then the president spoke his last words, "Goodbye, all; goodbye. It is God's way. His will be done. 'Nearer my God to Thee, nearer to Thee.'"[6] That hymn was played at his funeral, and it spoke of the heaven in which he so ardently believed and to which he looked forward:

> There let the way appear, step until Heav'n;
> All that Thou sendest me, in mercy given;
> Angels to beckon me nearer, my God, to Thee.
>
> There in my Father's home, safe and at rest,
> There in my Savior's love, perfectly blest;
> Age after age to be, nearer my God to Thee.[7]

At the Metropolitan Methodist Church in Washington, D.C., the Rev. W. H. Chapman gave a sermon at a special service for the president in which he spoke of William McKinley's strong and abiding Christian faith. While he was confident of McKinley's final destination, there was no talk about him looking down from heaven. There were, however, references to his being in heaven, conscious and enjoying the fellowship of believers who had gone before him. Chapman also admonished his congregation to live as faithfully to Christ as McKinley had in the way that people had spoken for decades about him:

> How peaceful and resigned he went into the valley, covered with splendid sunshine, and found rest from his labors! He has left behind him, to his kindred and to us the rich legacy of a splendid character and an unsullied record. A life that says to others: "This is the way. Walk in it, the way that leads to moral wealth, far above all material wealth, and which leads at last to heaven and to God."

> We shall miss him in this sanctuary and look no more upon him in yonder pew devotional in worship and listening attentively to the precious word as if indeed it were manna to his soul and a refreshing stream from the fountain of life. But he worshiped today in the temple not made with hands, with many of those with whom he was wont to worship in the church below. May we all imitate his example, emulate his virtues and at the last be counted worthy of a place with him in the kingdom of heaven.[8]

In a eulogy on September 19, the Hon. John W. Griggs also spoke about McKinley's deep spiritual character and his belief that the president's soul was at rest. These were important beliefs at the time, and Americans desired to hear them, especially in times of loss:

> But if President McKinley was noble in his life, in his death he was sublime.

> "He taught us how to live, (and O, too high The price of knowledge), taught us how to die." Shall we not rather see in him a manifestation of the greatness and the purity to which the Divine spirit that is in man may

attain when restrained and guided by the Divine standards? Shall we not hope, nay, believe! that, in a wider sphere, in a fairer land, his spirit still lives and labors and loves?

When darkness of death was settling over him he murmured words of rest and home. I think that when the light of the eternal morning greeted his soul's eyes, he knew that he had found them—rest and home.[9]

Most Americans were convinced that McKinley had gone to heaven, but they still had profound grief and sorrow over his tragic passing. Echoing the feelings of so many, Theodore Roosevelt told his close friend Henry Cabot Lodge how hard it was to believe that such a terrible thing could have happened in that progressive day and age:

You and I have lived too long, and have seen human nature from too many different sides, to be astounded at ordinary folly or ordinary wickedness, but it did not seem possible that at just this time in just this country, and in the case of this particular president, any human being could be so infamous a scoundrel, so crazy a fool as to attempt to assassinate him.[10]

Yet it had happened. The murder of William McKinley by an avowed anarchist was truly the "opening shot" of the new century.

∽o∽

The progress in science and technology that so many observers anticipated did come, and the developments—many that emerged right in 1900—eventually would change everyday life forever for the masses. There was Marie Curie's discovery that atoms could spontaneously break apart, releasing energy; Thomas Edison's inventing of nickel-alkaline storage batteries; the first zeppelin dirigibles appeared; and a new machine to detect earthquakes was created. Pioneering psychologist Sigmund Freud published his book *On the Interpretation of Dreams*. In 1903, the Wright Brothers made the first gas-motored and manned airplane, and Willis Carrier developed the air conditioner. The brilliant Albert Einstein published his theory of relativity, and automobiles were beginning to change the way people got from place to place, creating an increasingly more mobile society in the process. Although medicine lagged behind other fields, there were much-needed developments in sanitation, as well as the early stages of vaccinations against the scourge of disease.[11] Many Americans were already enjoying the benefits of electricity, automobiles, photography, and motion pictures, which provided entertainment for about thirty million of them weekly. Their family unit was stable, and divorce was rare. There was every reason to believe that the twentieth century would be a time of unprecedented human advancement.

∽o∾

Theological liberals continued to hope that the kingdom of God would come through social action, while Christians of orthodox and traditional convictions believed that saving souls from hell would result in a changed culture. There was, however, a very different movement afoot in American Christianity, one with roots in the very first century AD. It began on January 1, 1901, in Topeka, Kansas, when Agnes Ozman, a student at Bethel Bible College, received a gift of the Holy Spirit straight out of Acts 2—speaking in a language she couldn't understand. Most of the other students at Bethel also began speaking in tongues, as the phenomenon was called. Gifts of healing and prophecy followed.

Small-scale revivals spread to other places in the next four years, including Texas, North Carolina, and Minnesota. One man who hungered and thirsted for this "new" manifestation of the living God was a son of former slaves, the Rev. William J. Seymour. In 1906, a woman who visited Seymour's church in Houston invited him to speak to her congregation in Los Angeles. Initially, things went poorly because the elders charged that he had not yet spoken in tongues and was, therefore, unqualified to lead them in worship. Once Seymour and a small group of followers moved to a private home, however, he did speak in tongues, and a fresh wave of revival broke out. Moving to a bigger venue, at 312 Azusa Street, the congregants began to welcome three hundred to fifteen hundred people at a time who came from a variety of ages, ethnic, and social backgrounds. At those meetings, if a person felt led by the Holy Spirit to speak, he or she spoke regardless of social or theological pedigree. Services were ongoing nearly 24/7. Baptists, Quakers, and Presbyterians all felt drawn to the renewal—even a Jewish man who went there to gather information to use in sermons against Christians. According to Paul Strand:

> When he went up a staircase in the mission, a young lady pointed a finger at him and in perfect Hebrew—his native language—told his first name, last name, what he was doing in Los Angeles, and gave him a record of all his sins. He asked her where she learned Hebrew. She said she didn't know, she was just speaking in tongues. He fell to his knees and repented on the spot.[12]

This was the beginning of the modern Pentecostal movement. It was named after the events of Acts 2 when on the Day of Pentecost, followers of Jesus began to speak in other languages, and about three thousand people from around the known world were added to their fellowship. Like many other evangelical Christians, early twentieth-century Pentecostals held that a person had to repent of his sins and be baptized to newness of life in Christ Jesus; this was how one gained heaven and avoided hell. They regarded heaven and hell as literal places, both of them eternal, and looked forward to the second coming of Jesus. They promoted a strong moral code, as well as the authority of Scripture. Where they parted ways with other evangelicals was mostly in the arena of the miraculous, of "signs and wonders" like healings and prophecy. Pentecostals believed that those gifts did not end with the death of the first apostles but continued to the present time.

It's been widely reported that just before the worshipers moved to Azusa Street, a young person prophesied that a terrible earthquake was going to strike. Whether the prophecy was ever made is debatable, but if it was, the Pentecostals would have regarded it as a verification of God's mighty hand at work among them. The earthquake itself was a further blow to all who believed that the twentieth century was going to be heaven on earth.

∽o∼

Pietro Toresani, an Italian immigrant living in San Francisco, woke up abruptly at 5:12 a.m. on Wednesday, April 18, 1906. "There was a big noise as if it was made by the devil," he wrote in a journal. "There was a concert of bottles, 40 glasses, a mandolin and a guitar." He staggered out of his bed and wandered outside where "I lost courage and patience and evoking 'mommy' and 'daddy' repeatedly. . . . I threw myself again to the ground as if I had a disease, as if I was drunk. . . . Like a crazy man I was looking here and there at an infinity of dead bodies horribly squashed."[13]

W. E. Alexander recalled how he was literally shaken by the quake "until I thought my teeth would come out," while his bed bucked like a spooked horse.

> I never felt so small and helpless in my life as I did that morning when I gazed upon the stricken city. . . . When I looked out, the pale moon was shining through the smoke from the fires just starting and I halted in surprise, thinking, I suppose, that she should not be there; that by all tokens, she should have been shaken from her position and lain shattered and broken at our feet. We then went up on our roof and found that the fires were making great headway and my wife's first remark was "The city is doomed—no power on Earth can save it."[14]

Many people organized their dazed thoughts along religious lines; it was, after all, an event of "biblical proportions." A man named G. A. Raymond wandered around, trying to make sense of the terror as morning broke over the shattered city:

> Outside I witnessed a sight I never want to see again. It was dawn and light. I looked up. The air was filled with falling stones. People around me were crushed to death on all sides. All around the huge buildings were shaking and waving. Every moment there were reports like 100

cannons going off at one time. Then streams of fire would shoot out, and other reports followed.

I asked a man standing next to me what happened. Before he could answer a thousand bricks fell on him and he was killed. A woman threw her arms around my neck. I pushed her away and fled. All around me buildings were rocking and flames shooting. As I ran people on all sides were crying, praying and calling for help. I thought the end of the world had come.[15]

The quake was estimated at a 7.7 on the Richter Scale, with some saying it may have been as high as 8.3 in magnitude. When it rolled through the city, fires broke out, resulting in the worst urban inferno in U.S. history. Berkeley Professor H. Morse Stephens called it "One of the greatest conflagrations ever known."[16] The fires seethed for three days before they spent themselves, resulting in the destruction of 490 city blocks, homelessness for a quarter of a million people (out of a population of 400,000), and the deaths of between 450 and 700 souls. Estimates of the damage surpassed $350,000,000.[17]

Human achievement and advancement, no matter how impressive, had not been able to prevent the cataclysm.

∽∘∾

By 1910, McKinley's assassination and the San Francisco earthquake were becoming distant memories. More sanguine observers of the American scene, including increasing numbers of secular modernists, continued to hope that the twentieth century would be a golden age in human history. Of them, D. A. Carson says, "In its most optimistic form, modernism held that ultimately knowledge would revolutionize the world, squeeze God to the periphery or perhaps abandon him to his own devices, and build an edifice of glorious knowledge to the great God Science."[18] Perhaps the proudest human achievement of all was a fantastic new ship that appeared on the scene in 1912, a luxury vessel that would dwarf a modern airplane. *Shipbuilder* magazine called it "practically unsinkable." In *A Night to Remember*, Walter Lord said that a deckhand, trying to soothe the fears of one passenger, told her, "Not even God could sink her."[19] But sink she did. According to James Galyon:

> Despite the absolute faith that some had in science and technology at the beginning of the twentieth century, the Titanic struck an iceberg on Sunday, April 14, at 11:40 p.m. Having been lauded as the safest ship ever built, the Titanic carried only 20 lifeboats, not enough to accommodate even half of her 2,200 passengers and crew. Less than two hours after striking the iceberg, the Titanic sunk. That morning of April 15, the Carpathia rescued 705 survivors. 1,522 passengers and crew had been lost.[20]

It came as a surprise to some that, unlike God, modern technology was not infallible.

∽∘∾

In February 1914 there were more than thirty organizations in the United States promoting world peace. Industrialist Andrew Carnegie was so optimistic that he created a two-million-dollar endowment for a "Church Peace Union" with a directive for alternate use of the funds if peace did become "fully established."[21] On June 28, Carnegie's dream began to unravel in distant Sarajevo. The Archduke Francis Ferdinand, heir to the throne of the Austro-Hungarian Empire, was on a state visit with his wife, the Duchess Sophie Chotek. As they rode in an open car, a Serbian student opened fire, killing them both. Austria-Hungary declared war on Serbia, followed by Russia's military mobilization. Germany declared war on Russia, then on Russia's ally, France. When Germany invaded Belgium, England declared war on Germany.

Europeans initially met the war with much chest thumping. They believed that the troops would be home by Christmas, but the traditional war strategy of massed infantry charges supported by artillery failed in this new era. Instead, entire nations mobilized their resources and hurled them at one another. Industrialization had changed the technique

of war so that man was now the slave, not the master, of the weapons
he had created—machine guns, poison gases, airplanes, tanks, and sub-
marines. Americans largely desired to remain neutral in the conflict; it
seemed a localized affair, and the United States hadn't yet become a true
world power. Over the next three years, however, they watched in alarm
as Europe ravaged itself. By 1915, two-and-a-half million Russian soldiers were dead, along with 20 percent of the country's civilians. In 1917,
when the continent seemed on the brink of either a communist takeover
or total destruction, the United States entered the war. In his address to
Congress, President Woodrow Wilson said, "The world must be safe for
democracy." Historian William Leuchtenburg believes that there was a
deeper, more spiritual reason for our declaration of war that reflected
the state of the overall culture:

> American entrance into the war cannot be seen apart from the
> American sense of mission. The United States believed that American
> moral idealism could be extended outward, that American Christian
> democratic ideals could and should be universally applied. . . . The
> culmination of a long political tradition of emphasis on sacrifice and
> decisive moral combat, the war was embraced as that final struggle
> where the righteous would do battle for the Lord.[22]

Washington, D.C., pastor Randolph H. McKim told his parishioners
that this was a holy crusade of the highest magnitude, that it was God
Himself who had "summoned us to this war." He said that the war was
history's greatest crusade, a holy war, because our Christian nation was
engaged in a struggle "with this unholy and blasphemous power."[23] Ironi-
cally, that "unholy and blasphemous power" was Germany, the land that
had "tutored" America in theology, art, and philosophy over much of the
nineteenth century.[24]

Many American leaders, both secular and religious, viciously attacked almost everything German. The refined Presbyterian pastor
Henry van Dyke called Germany's Kaiser Wilhelm the "Potsdam Were-
wolf," and Boston's Courtland Meyers proclaimed, "If the Kaiser is a

Christian, the devil in hell is a Christian, and I am an atheist."[25] Newell
Dwight Hillis, of Brooklyn's Plymouth Church, actually called for the
extermination of the German people and the sterilization of its soldiers.
"That Germans were all 'swinish Huns' became a cliché of the American
pulpit."[26] In a very uncomplicated way, this was true for both liberals
and the more traditional and orthodox churches. Virtually all of them
united around the belief that the global war had to be won by the forces
of heaven, with which America was aligned, and not the forces of hell.
Perhaps even more ironic is that German higher criticism, which was
causing so much conflict within American churches, was not rejected
outright during the war.

∽•∾

At the time of the Armistice, November 11, 1918, a total of twenty million people had been wounded and thousands of them maimed by the
new weapons of mass destruction. Ten million Europeans had died—
6,000 for each day of the war; 116,516 Americans had lost their lives,
and another 204,000 had been wounded. The material losses were so as-
tronomical as to be inconceivable. The war had involved thirty sovereign
states and brought about the end of the Russian, Ottoman, German, and
Hapsburg Empires. France lost half of its men between the ages of twenty
and thirty-two. Of those who served from England's Oxford University,
20 percent died. Europe's future was impoverished. Pat Robertson was
right when he referred to the war as "four years of terror and carnage beyond anything the human mind could have imagined, certainly not the
minds of those who anticipated that the 20th century would be heaven on
earth."[27]

A LOST
GENERATION

Walked eye-deep in hell
believing in old men's lies, then unbelieving
came home, home to a lie,
home to deceits,
home to old lies and new infamy...[1]

EZRA POUND

Many of those who emerged from the wreckage of World War I thought they had passed through a hellish experience, while paradoxically no longer actually believing in hell. The devastation and disillusionment of the hostilities, as well as the influence of modern thinkers like Friedrich Nietzsche and Sigmund Freud, had made a profound impact on this generation of lost souls. Shortly before the Great War, Nietzsche had proclaimed that religious leaders and other authority figures had used the idea of hell as a "bizarre supernatural threat" to keep people in line. Similarly, Freud asserted that all religion and its doctrines could be categorized as "institutionalized neurosis."[2] Society's moorings were coming undone, even in America, which had emerged from the war as a world power. One voice of that era, W. B. Yeats, wrote two years after the Treaty of Versailles:

Turning and turning in the widening gyre
The falcon cannot hear the falconer;
Things fall apart; the centre cannot hold;

Mere anarchy is loosed upon the world,
The blood-dimmed tide is loosed, and everywhere
The ceremony of innocence is drowned;
The best lack all conviction, while the worst
Are full of passionate intensity.[3]

The 1920s may be known today as "the Roaring Twenties" and the "Jazz Age," but it was also a decade of disillusionment, not just for war-weary Europeans and intellectuals, but also for the masses in America. Sydney Ahlstrom explains:

> The Armistice of 1918 ended the fighting, but the Great War had so shaken the world that for a whole generation most of the human race lived in its shadow. Americans sought desperately to escape from its influence, tried almost to deny that it had occurred. Yet every aspect of their lives in the postwar years reflected its baneful impact. Convinced that they had made a terrible mistake by going to war, a great many Americans rejected the values that had led them to do so. Idealism gave way to materialism, naiveté to cynicism, moral purposefulness to irresponsibility, faith to iconoclasm. . . . All society seemed in flux.[4]

The writers of that time expressed the fears and failings of humanity in stark terms, and rose to positions of authority. The old arbiters of society, the politicians and clergy, seemed painfully out of touch with the new reality. The liberals had misread the times' signs by prophesying peace when there clearly was no peace, and the conservative traditionalists were on the defensive against challenges from science and the humanities. In "The Hollow Men," T. S. Eliot expressed the spirit of the age.

We are the hollow men
We are the stuffed men
Leaning together
Headpiece filled with straw. Alas!
Our dried voices, when
We whisper together
Are quiet and meaningless
As wind in dry grass

Or rats' feet over broken glass
In our dry cellar.

. . . .

This is the dead land
This is cactus land
Here the stone images
Are raised, here they receive
The supplication of a dead man's hand
Under the twinkle of a fading star.

. . . .

This is the way the world ends
This is the way the world ends
This is the way the world ends
Not with a bang but a whimper [5]

The war shattered the old social order, leaving many without a sense of purpose or a moral compass by which to steer their lives. In the aftermath of the conflict, many writers looked to the newly created Soviet Union for direction, since its atheistic philosophy of communist socialism appeared to be working. Why not, they thought, eradicate the beliefs and traditions that obviously hadn't succeeded, especially Christianity and capitalism, and try something new?

At times those writers openly jeered at the Christian religion, like Sinclair Lewis who, in 1925, published *Elmer Gantry*, the story of a ne'er-do-well who decided that the easiest way to make a living was to peddle Christianity. On the side he caroused with women. Billy Sunday and other evangelical leaders condemned the novel, but it became a commercial success and enjoyed a wide following on stage, and on the screen in later adaptations.

While the major literary figures of 1920s America mocked both Christian beliefs and the democratic system, one of them surprised the world when he actually became a professing Christian. While living in England in 1927, T. S. Eliot went public with his declaration of faith in Jesus Christ and joined the Anglican Church. His first key work after that, *Ash Wednesday*, speaks of his wrestling with God and what it was like to embrace faith after living in disbelief. Many of his contemporaries expressed their disappointment that Eliot had gone Christian, but it couldn't have come as a complete surprise. He had long been contemplating faith issues. For example, in "The Waste Land" he had employed imagery from Dante's *Inferno* to describe the people standing at the entrance to hell.

∽∘∾

As people groped to understand life in an unfamiliar landscape, the way they thought about the afterlife changed. One major contributor to that shift was Roman Catholicism, whose numbers were steadily rising in America. Immigrants and their offspring were beginning to exert considerable influence on the American mind-set about heaven and hell as Catholics began to hold major positions of leadership. Among them were Irish Catholic John Fitzgerald, Boston's mayor in the previous decade and grandfather of John F. Kennedy, and Al Smith, who in 1928 became the first Catholic to run for president. This increased the social standing of other Catholics and made the teachings and practices of their communion more mainstream, particularly the doctrine of purgatory, where the devout are cleansed and prepared for heaven. They also popularized the idea of praying to deceased saints and the Virgin Mary. These may have struck Protestants as peculiar, even questionable, but it also gave people the idea that the living might just be able to connect with the dead, who obviously were in a conscious state, and who could possibly intervene on their behalf. This, combined with the teachings of spiritualism that had begun in the mid-nineteenth century, gave many people a feeling that the dead were aware of what was going on with the living.

In this era, Christian theology as a whole had swung from a theocentric view of heaven to one more oriented around people and their earthly relationships. In this newer version, believers in Christ—or all good people, according to most liberals—would be reunited with loved ones in heaven and enjoy a perfected form of the life they'd known on earth. The culture promoted the idea that people could do as they pleased, and God wouldn't really mind all that much. They could drink bootlegged whiskey, shorten their skirts, bob their hair, smoke, dance, and joyride without worrying about eternal consequences.

After Prohibition became law in 1920, the quest for liquor went underground, and organized crime played a major role in its production and distribution. Secretive bars known as speakeasies sprang up, their owners notorious for bribing the police and other law-enforcement officials to look the other way. Likewise, there was an expectation that God—if there even were one—would look the other way, too, both in this world and in the next. Were there really such things, many wondered, as heavenly rewards and hellish punishments, or was that just part of a fading and discredited system? The acerbic journalist H. L. Mencken observed in 1924 that Christendom "may be defined briefly as that part of the world in which, if any man stands up in public and solemnly swears he is a Christian, all his auditors will laugh." Another writer, Joseph Wood Krutch, remarked, "Both our practical morality and our emotional lives are adjusted to a world that no longer exists."[6]

America's national religion, Protestantism, was also in flux with the changing times as some leaders pledged their allegiance to the old, standard beliefs about heaven and hell while others came out in favor of a more "modern," benevolent interpretation, resulting in a major confrontation between fundamentalism and modernism. Initially, the term "fundamentalist" referred simply to the defenders of traditional, orthodox Christianity—actually those who had been at the forefront of mainstream Protestantism throughout American history. George Marsden observes that their "most alarming experience was that of finding themselves living in a culture that by the 1920s was openly turning away from God."[7] At the heart of modernism lay the theory of evolution, and many avant-garde thinkers created the stereotype of fundamentalists as ignorant hayseeds who decried science and reason in an ill-conceived effort to prove, once again, that the world was flat. Reality, however, did not always match that pigeonhole.

The most well known guardian of Christian orthodoxy in the 1920s was a brilliant New Testament scholar from Princeton Theological Seminary, hardly a bastion of the dimwitted. J. Gresham Machen was born in 1881 in Baltimore, a son of privilege and culture who graduated from Johns Hopkins University before going on to further studies at both Princeton Seminary and Princeton University. During his graduate years, Machen spent time in Germany where he was exposed to its theological liberalism and underwent a faith crisis. Upon his return to Princeton, his doubts were erased by B. B. Warfield and Francis Patton, who helped him reaffirm orthodox Christianity. Machen became a New Testament professor at the seminary. He disliked the term "fundamentalist" because he said it sounded like something new when, in fact, it was a reaffirmation of historic Christianity. In his classic 1923 book *Christianity and Liberalism*, Machen made a case that modernist theology wasn't even Christian:

> We shall be interested in showing that despite the liberal use of
> traditional phraseology modern liberalism not only is a different religion
> from Christianity but belongs in a totally different class of religions....
> Our principle concern just now is to show that the liberal attempt at
> reconciling Christianity with modern science has really relinquished
> everything distinctive about Christianity, so that what remains is in
> essentials only that same indefinite type of religious aspiration which
> was in the world before Christianity came upon the scene.[8]

As fundamentalism gained strength, new institutions of higher learning organized to promote the faith, including the National Bible Institute of Philadelphia (now Philadelphia Biblical University) and BIOLA (Bible Institute of Los Angeles, now Biola University). Their statements of faith provide a general idea regarding "fundamentalist" teachings about heaven and hell, which were oriented along classical Christian lines with a decidedly premillenial orientation. According to Biola:

All those who receive Jesus Christ as their Savior and their Lord, and who confess Him as such before their fellow men, become children of God and receive eternal life. They become heirs of God and joint-heirs with Jesus Christ. At death their spirits depart to be with Christ in conscious blessedness, and at the Second Coming of Christ their bodies shall be raised and transformed into the likeness of the body of His glory.

All those who persistently reject Jesus Christ in the present life shall be raised from the dead and throughout eternity exist in the state of conscious, unutterable, endless torment of anguish. . . .

There is a personal devil, a being of great cunning and power: "The prince of the power of the air," "The prince of this world," "The god of this age." He can exert vast power only so far as God suffers him to do so. He shall ultimately be cast into the lake of fire and brimstone and shall be tormented day and night forever.[9]

Philadelphia Biblical University's position is similar, though stated more briefly: "We believe that both believers and unbelievers will be raised from the dead bodily, believers to conscious eternal blessedness in God's presence and unbelievers to conscious eternal punishment and separation from Him."[10]

∞

Modernism's most popular spokesman in the 1920s was the pastor Harry Emerson Fosdick, who came up through the Baptist tradition before becoming a Presbyterian minister. A graduate of Colgate, he received theological training at Union Seminary in New York, which was a major center for liberalism. Fosdick boasted that he'd never recited the Apostles' Creed, and he repudiated the virgin birth, scriptural inerrancy, and the second coming saying, "The Lord [is] to be found in living experience . . . not at the end of some creed."[11] He claimed that he wanted modernists to live peacefully with fundamentalists, but he couldn't seem to stop himself from taking potshots at his detractors. When he delivered a sermon, "Shall the Fundamentalists Win?" in 1922, he stated that the

Bible, rather than being God's inerrant Word, instead gave an account of God's ongoing work in the world. He was brought up for charges of heresy, but resigned his pulpit before the trial's completion. The message that stirred up all of the trouble so impressed oil baron John D. Rockefeller that he paid to have it printed and distributed to all the Protestant clergy in the United States. He also went on to help finance the building of Riverside Church in Manhattan, an independent institution from which Fosdick presided in an increasingly popular ministry of preaching and publishing.

Though Fosdick was a modernist, his views about heaven and hell were unexpected for someone of that school of thought. On the one hand, he disparaged Jonathan Edwards's Calvinist beliefs as portraying a cruel God who tortured most of the human race in hell forever. On the other, he bemoaned that modern believers didn't take sin seriously enough. Most liberals like Fosdick believed that there were other ways to salvation and heaven, as well as of understanding ultimate consequences for sin, than the traditional ones.[12] He didn't believe God would "torture" unrepentant sinners forever, but that they would suffer the natural consequences of their own sin. To him, a loving God would admit most people to heaven. Nevertheless, he expressed concern that perhaps Americans had gone from one extreme to another in their afterlife views, that maybe they were thinking of God as being *too* benevolent:

> Jonathan Edwards' Enfield sermon pictured sinners held over the blazing abyss of hell in the hands of a wrathful deity who at any moment was likely to let go, and so terrific was that discourse in its delivery that women fainted and strong men clung in agony to the pillars of the church. Obviously, we do not believe in that kind of God any more, and as always in reaction we swing to the opposite extreme, so in the theology of these recent years we have taught a very mild, benignant sort of deity. One of our popular drinking songs sums up this aspect of our new theology:

> "God is not censorious / When His children have their fling."

Indeed, the god of the new theology has not seemed to care acutely about sin; certainly he has not been warranted to punish heavily; he has been an indulgent parent and when we have sinned, a polite "Excuse me" has seemed more than adequate to make amends.[13]

~•~

Back in the Middle Ages, theology was the "queen of the sciences" and the final authority in all matters pertaining to life and death. If there was a question about the afterlife, a person consulted the church and the Bible for answers. If someone wondered why sickness happened, he looked to the Bible. If there was a question about nature, the answer had to be theological. Why did water travel downhill? Because God wanted it to be that way. Every question had to be settled theologically. The sun rose in the east because God made it so. If there was a disagreement between math and Scripture, math was wrong. Scripture was *the* authority for everything.

With the coming of the industrial and scientific revolutions, there was more of a compartmentalization of authority. How fast an object fell to the ground was considered a scientific question. Likewise, how trees grew and how the solar system operated were to be handled scientifically. Questions of ultimate importance, such as where we came from and where we were going when we died, were theological, religious questions. At that time, science and theology were viewed mainly on equal footing; they had their own set of rules. Whichever realm the matter belonged to was authoritative in that matter.

In the 1920s at the time of the media frenzy over the so-called "Scopes Monkey Trial," there came a watershed in American thought. Suddenly science became the authority on everything, including life's origins and what would happen when we died. No longer was religion about truth, it was a matter of personal opinion that also had to submit to science's dominion.

The Scopes trial was a classic battle between fundamentalism and modernism that took place because teacher John Scopes broke a Tennessee statute by teaching evolution at Dayton's Rhea County High School. The American Civil Liberties Union (ACLU) had announced earlier that it was willing to fund a test case of the new law, and Scopes, though initially reluctant, decided to participate. The ensuing trial brought a circus atmosphere to the small town as the popular but fading politician/orator William Jennings Bryan prosecuted the case, and the acclaimed ACLU attorney Clarence Darrow defended Scopes. Darrow believed the outcome of the trial would have sweeping repercussions for human history: "Scopes isn't on trial," he said. "Civilization is on trial. The prosecution is opening the doors for a reign of bigotry equal to anything in the Middle Ages. No man's belief will be safe if they win."[14]

He was joined by the caustic H. L. Mencken, who covered the trial for *The Baltimore Sun* and who openly despised Christians. He especially thought of orthodox believers as "*Homo boobiens*" who believed in imbecilic doctrines. Doug Linder believes that "Mencken shaped, as well as reported, the Scopes trial," frequently offering Darrow and the defense team his advice. He urged them to "make a fool out of Bryan" and all that he stood for.[15] The journalist cruelly attacked Bryan in print, charging that the old statesman dreamed of "a world unanimously sure of Heaven and unanimously idiotic on this earth." Likewise, Mencken claimed that Bryan wanted to be "the peasants' Pope" and to "shake and inflame these poor ignoramuses." He concluded, "It is tragedy indeed, to begin life as a hero and to end it as a buffoon."[16] Throughout the trial, he and Darrow seized every opportunity to diminish Bryan and Christianity. After eight brutally hot days, the trial ended when the jury found Scopes guilty and fined him $100. Mencken believed that in spite of the verdict, the trial had been a great victory for the forces of progress and modernism over antiquated, outdated Christianity.

At church on the Sunday after the trial, Bryan offered the prayer, concluding with the words of a favorite hymn, "Faith of our fathers, holy faith. We will be true to Thee till death." After lunch with his wife and a few phone calls, he lay down for a nap from which he never awakened.[17] Upon hearing the news, H. L. Mencken said: "God aimed at Darrow, missed, and hit Bryan instead." He also made a snide remark that it wasn't Bryan's heart that had killed him, but his stomach.[18] Scopes said, "I could sense an opinion forming that Bryan was a martyr who had died defending the Grand Old Fundamental Religion."[19] Bryan's death brought about a national outpouring of respect and grief, as well as an attempt by some modern thinkers to distance themselves from Mencken and Darrow. Walter Lippman of the *New York World* wrote, "The truth is that when Mr. Darrow in his anxiety to humiliate and ridicule Mr. Bryan resorted to sneering and scoffing at the Bible he convinced millions who act on superficial impressions that Bryan is right in his assertion that the contest at Dayton was for and against the Christian religion." Even the humanist scholar Edwin Mims said, "When Clarence Darrow is put forth as the champion of the forces of enlightenment to fight the battle for scientific knowledge, one feels almost persuaded to become a Fundamentalist."[20]

Columbia Records released a country ballad the year of Bryan's death honoring the man for his efforts to uphold historic Christianity and declaring its faith in the statesman's whereabouts:

> There he fought for what was righteous and the battle it was won,
> Then the Lord called him to heaven for his work on earth was done.[21]

Bryan's desire to be a good Christian soldier and his hope in heaven gave him peace of mind, even when enemies assailed him. The first line of his will echoes his serenity. It read: "In the name of God, farewell. Trusting for my salvation to the blood of Jesus Christ, my Lord and Redeemer, and relying on his promise for my hope of resurrection, I consign my body to the dust and commend my spirit to God who gave it."[22]

Darrow's end wasn't nearly as placid. Shortly before his death in 1938, Darrow received a visitor whose life's ambition was to meet the great attorney. Dr. John Herman asked Darrow, "Now that you've come this far in life . . . how would you sum up your life?" Darrow walked over to a coffee table and picked up a Bible, surprising Herman since Darrow had spent most of his life ridiculing it. "This verse in the Bible describes my life," the lawyer said, opening to Luke 5:5. Changing the "we" to "I," he read aloud, "I have toiled all the night and have taken nothing." Then he put the Bible down and caught Herman's eye. "I have lived a life without purpose," he said, "without meaning, without direction. I don't know where I came from. And I don't know what I'm doing here. And worst of all, I don't know what's going to happen to me when I punch out of here."[23]

13

DEPRESSION AND THE
GOOD WAR

When people think of the 1930s, images usually arise of unemployment and bread lines, hobos bumming cigarettes and train rides, and the Dust Bowl. It was also the age when the secular mass media began to dominate American life. For example, as strapped for cash as they were, by the end of the decade some 80 percent of Americans owned radios, and seventy-five million went to the movies weekly. Radio, movies, and newspapers both reflected and helped shape the culture of that time, supplanting the church as the keeper of the keys to the American way of life. What Americans listened to and watched were aimed for the lowest common denominator in terms of intellectual content, good taste, and morals, and their influence was enormous. "Inevitably," John Garraty says, "the mores and vocabulary of the movies were imitated by those to whom they represented the fulfillment of every ambition. They set the popular fashion in dress, home furnishings, play, morals, even in marriage and family life; and increasingly human nature came to conform to commercial art."[1]

During the Depression, movies and radio programs also served as therapy, whereas in other times, people had turned to the church, the Bible, and fellow believers for comfort and strength. Never before, however, had a constant source of mass entertainment been available to them, and now it served both to soothe and distract. Hollywood gave an occasional nod to religious subjects, turning out films like *The Crusades*, *The Sign of the Cross*, and *Dante's Inferno*, but producers paid far more attention to monsters, musicals, and screwball comedies, often pushing the envelope of established morals and good taste. Mostly, says Sydney Ahlstrom, "the Hollywood star system mocked the older moral standards, both Catholic and Protestant."[2]

Prior to the 1930s, in cases where death was a public matter, it was handled from a Christian faith perspective (one that included a firm belief in heaven and hell) in church services, funerals, and newspaper articles. There were usually comments about the deceased person's faithfulness to God and the heavenly reward that awaited him or her. There often was an admonition to emulate the person of faith or to seek comfort in God alone. A brief look at how the media handled death-related stories in the 1930s, however, demonstrates how the times had changed.

When Texas lawmen gunned down the notorious outlaws Bonnie and Clyde in May of 1934, the news focused on the pair's killing sprees and how they got what they deserved, not what they were going to get in the afterlife. Stories about the kidnapping and murder of Charles and Anne Morrow Lindbergh's baby in 1932 focused on the odious nature of the crime and the public's outrage. Similarly, when the German airship *Hindenburg* burst into flames while landing at Lakehurst, New Jersey, in 1937, there wasn't an attempt to urge the public to always be ready to meet their Maker, but an emphasis on the actual disaster apart from any meaning for the living or the dead.

Just as theology had once been the "queen of the sciences," the eminence of religion in America had waned significantly by the 1930s. In 1933, William Kelley Wright of Dartmouth College observed, "Today we are passing through a period of religious depression not less severe than the concomitant moral and economic depression."[3] Ministers in the traditionally "mainline" churches especially suffered from low morale "as they saw their Protestant culture disintegrate under their eyes."[4]

Intellectuals in the '30s had strong inclinations toward communism, with its atheistic philosophy. "Editors and lawyers like H. L. Mencken and Clarence Darrow," Martin Marty says, "were joined by a generation of novelists like Sinclair Lewis and Ernest Hemingway, who saw no positive place for the churches. The academic-intellectual style wavered between mere agnosticism on one hand and satiric or vitriolic rejection on the other."[5]

The churches that had once championed historic, orthodox Christianity had marginalized themselves by trying to accommodate modernism and liberalism. On the defensive, no longer sure of their core beliefs, "blown here and there by every wind of teaching" (Ephesians 4:14), "mainline" churches began a long, slow fade from national influence that continues to this day. There was among its leaders and members a creeping universalism and a belief that maybe other religions also offered ways to God. Suddenly, doing missions work to save the souls of people who did not know Jesus didn't seem as urgent as it once did. Surely God wouldn't consign someone to hell just because he or she had never heard of Christ.

∞°∞

In that hostile environment a new theology emerged known as neo-orthodoxy in which thinkers like brothers Reinhold and Richard Niebuhr, Paul Tillich, and Karl Barth rethought classical Christian teachings and the Scriptures within the context of the modern world. In *The Church Against the World* (1935), H. Richard Niebuhr called for Christians to return to the Bible, and he tried to reconcile certain troublesome doctrines of the ancient church with modern times, including those about hell. "Preaching about hell is always resented by men of so-called liberal mind," he wrote. "How could the infliction of torment be rhymed with the rule of a merciful God? What human wickedness deserved such a consequence?"[6] His brother, Reinhold, said that in our finitude, humans cannot describe "the furniture of heaven and the temperature of hell . . . or be too certain about any details of the kingdom of God in which history is consummated."[7] Karl Barth suggested that in former days Christians thought not many people would get to heaven; but now he wondered, why couldn't it actually be the other way around? In *Hell Under Fire*, Christopher W. Morgan and Robert A. Peterson recount, "Barth came to the theological conclusion that evil was fundamentally a negation ... and held out hope that the victory of God in Christ would extend to a universal redemption and reconciliation. Hell would be no more."[8]

In the 1930s, denominations that equivocated about heaven and especially hell lost members, influence, and money, but churches that championed historic, orthodox Christianity—in other words, the beliefs that had dominated American life and thought until after the Civil War—thrived. Now labeled "fundamentalist," they experienced significant increases in attendence in the Depression era. According to Joel Carpenter:

> During the 1930s and 1940s ... fundamentalists ... establish[ed] their
> identity, consolidate[d] an institutional network, and [rethought] their
> mission to America. Ironically, they were freed by their defeats in the
> antimodernist controversies to concentrate on these more positive tasks.
> While they were predicting the world's imminent demise and building a
> subculture to protect themselves from worldly society, fundamentalists
> were also retooling their evangelistic techniques and seizing upon
> inviting cultural trends to mount a renewed public presence. Their goals
> were time-honored evangelical ones: to bring revival to America and the
> gospel to the world.[9]

Even during the financial challenges of the Depression, twenty-six new "fundamentalist" schools were established, including Dallas Theological Seminary and Bob Jones University; Wheaton College in Illinois was the fastest growing of all liberal arts schools in America during much of the decade. In addition, evangelical publications increased in circulation, their mission agencies grew, and summer Bible conferences flourished. By the end of the 1930s, conservative Christian churches increased in membership while the mainline denominations struggled.

∽०∾

In early December 1941, Dr. Peter Marshall felt that he couldn't preach the message he'd prepared for midshipmen at the United States Naval Academy. "All the preceding week he had been haunted by a strange feeling that he should change his announced topic and preach a particular sermon," wrote his wife, Catherine. "It was a feeling he could not shake off . . . so Peter preached on the text, seemingly a strange text for young midshipmen: "For what is your life? It is even a vapour, that appeareth for a little time and then vanisheth away (James 4:14)."[10] While driving back to their home in Washington, D.C., later that afternoon, Peter and Catherine Marshall listened as a radio announcer interrupted with a grave announcement: the Japanese had bombed the United States naval fleet at Pearl Harbor. On the day that President Roosevelt said would "live in infamy," almost twenty-four hundred American servicemen died, and nearly 1,200 were wounded. America declared war on Japan, as well as its allies, Germany and Italy.

World War I had seemed to most Americans an internecine power struggle between cousins over the family fortune. World War II, on the other hand, clearly presented itself as a conflict between good and evil as Germany decimated Europe, slaughtering Jews and other people it determined were undesirable amongst its "master race." Japan was conducting its own march of death in Asia and the Pacific to the glory of its emperor-god, Hirohito, murdering foreigners and dissidents, and turning women into sex slaves. As in the first global war, American churches supported the effort with countless volunteer activities like offering "canteen" programs for the servicemen, preparing medical supplies, and lending their clergy as chaplains. But there were significant differences. Gone was the vitriol hurled against the enemy during the first conflict. Gone also was the great influence that churches had exerted a generation earlier upon the society. Nevertheless, there was, according to Ken Burns, "A spontaneous combustion that took place. . . . We were

surprised [when creating the documentary series *The War*] at the amount
of communion footage we saw. Some sergeant got down on his knees.
. . . There were services on decks of ships, just an amazing manifestation
of religiousness in a more cynical period."[11] Yet the religiousness had a
different feel to it than in past wars. There weren't full-scale revivals like
the ones during the Civil War, for example, and most of the fighting men
didn't have the rock-solid orthodox beliefs of their ancestors. Even so,
countless troops did turn to God for help. Of them, Tom Brokaw writes:

> Faith in God was not a casual part of the lives of the World War II
> generation. The men and women who went off to war, or stayed home,
> volunteer that their spiritual beliefs helped them cope with the constant
> presence of possible death, serious injury, or the other anxieties
> attendant to the disruptions brought on by war. . . .
>
> On the front lines, chaplains were not incidental to the war effort. Some
> jumped with the Airborne troops of D-Day and others risked their own
> lives to administer last rites or other comforting words to dying and
> grievously wounded young men wherever the battle took them. The
> very nature of war prompted many who participated in it to think more
> deeply about God and their relationship to a higher being once they
> returned home.[12]

One of those men was Harry Reginald "Reg" Hammond, who said,
"I think we were on God's side. The United States has done some foolish
things, but in that war I knew we had God with us."[13] When he fought
on D-Day at Normandy, he "saw more bodies in a short time than most
undertakers will see in a lifetime. Young men dead alongside the road.
Every night I would pray for those guys and myself. I think it deepened
my faith. . . . You needed something to keep you going. . . . It made me realize that there was something much larger than just me. I realized it had
to be God."[14] Many years after the war, Hammond became a minister.

Former U.S. Senator Mark Hatfield was a young man who saw action at Iwo Jima, and he reflected on what it meant to face death and the
hereafter. "I was raised in a very strong Christian home," he said. "I sup-

pose that was also part of my armor, in the sense that if I got hit, I knew where I was headed. I had confidence in my faith."[15]

Corporal Charles White of Chicago served in the European theater of the war. He said, "During my duty in the Army I was often afraid, but I took comfort in my awareness of my honor and loyalty to God and country. I had no time to worry about my afterlife. It would do no good since no matter what I did, I would be judged in the afterlife by God, who would add up my score and tell me."[16]

∽o∽

In those years, a new conviction developed, however unarticulated, that someone who died in such a noble undertaking couldn't possibly go to hell. After all, God was so obviously on the side of the Allies, who were fighting to save civilization from the barbarism of Hitler, Imperial Japan, and Mussolini. *They* were the bad guys, them and their evil cohorts, Tojo, Goering, Hess—they were the ones assigned to everlasting perdition. Moreover, the Allied soldiers had already been through the worst experiences imaginable, so how could hell be any worse? This was echoed in the epitaph that a war correspondent at Guadalcanal found on a headstone in the marine cemetery:

> And when he gets to heaven
> To St. Peter he will tell,
> One more Marine reporting, sir—
> I've served my time in hell.[17]

Catholic chaplain Father Joseph Barry saw matters differently. He thought the terrible experiences his men had faced might just keep them from going to the bad place. He served in Italy during a period when the Germans were bombing the American position all night long in order to disorient them and render their fighting ineffective the next day. Death always seemed close to those men, and Father Barry said the constant noise and threat of dying had the salutary effect of catalyzing their faith:

"Each shell came a little closer, and . . . each prayer became a little more fervent."[18]

As Ken Burns discovered during his massive interviews with World War II veterans, it wasn't uncommon for them not to be thinking about God or the afterlife, however, in the heat of battle itself. Wilfred "Mac" McCarty was wounded at the Battle of the Bulge, and this was true for him, although he was a practicing Catholic:

> A German 88 shell and I shared the same space in the Battle of the Bulge in Belgium. I thought I was going to die, and I did not think about Heaven or Hell, but in the confusion I was trying to figure out what country I was dying in. Was it Luxemburg, still France, Liechtenstein or one of those small countries? It became very important to me. It was Belgium. While I was constantly praying, I wasn't at the time. I had a prayer book that had a tin cover on it in my pocket for some reason. A bullet could easily have gone through the tin, and that would have been no protection, but you don't always think logically. I also had religious medals around my neck to play it safe. But to tell the truth, at the moment of crisis I was not thinking of God, but he must have been thinking of me as I did not die. I was operated on in the field, sent back to England for further operations, and then had to go back as combat soldiers were needed.[19]

⌁

Many were keenly aware of their dependence on God as the Allied forces of the United States, Great Britain, and Canada prepared to invade Europe via Normandy, France, on the morning of June 6, 1944. Nearly five thousand Americans would die that day. The night before, General Dwight Eisenhower visited some of the soldiers, asking where they came from, dreading what lay ahead for them. Seeing the general frown, one paratrooper assured him, "Now quit worrying, General, we'll take care of this thing for you."[20] In his invasion field order to the troops, he was blunt about what they would face. "Your enemy is well trained, well equipped and battle-hardened. He will fight savagely. . . . [Therefore] beseech the blessings of Almighty God on this great and noble undertaking."[21]

A colonel in the 101st Airborne Division told his men the night before, "Men, get on your knees. Now I'm not a religious man, but I want you to get on your knees." Then he prayed briefly for them. He died in the first wave.[22]

President Roosevelt also led the nation in prayer, mentioning that death would claim many and foreseeing, in keeping with the tone of the day, that they would go to heaven:

> Almighty God: Our sons, pride of our nation, this day have set upon
> a mighty endeavor, a struggle to preserve our Republic, our religion,
> and our civilization, and to set free a suffering humanity. Lead them
> straight and true; give strength to their arms, stoutness to their hearts,
> steadfastness in their faith. They will need Thy blessings. . . . Some will
> never return. Embrace these, Father, and receive them, Thy heroic
> servants, into Thy kingdom.[23]

A paratrooper sat in his plane with his rosary, vowing that he'd never violate the sixth commandment again. His buddy prayed, "Lord, please don't let me get anybody killed and don't let me get killed either. I really think I'm too young for this."

Another repeatedly asked God, "Give me guts, give me guts."[24] Each in his own way tried to make peace with God, knowing he might be meeting Him very soon.

∽o∾

The Allies were victorious on D-Day, although thousands of Americans lost their lives trying to drive the Nazis back. The war continued for another year after that, ending in some of the most unspeakable horrors the world had ever faced. When the Allies liberated the German death camps, they uncovered the shocking truth that nine million people, two-thirds of them Jews, had been murdered just for being who they were. Most of them had perished in gas chambers and ovens. The Japanese had vowed to fight to the death, taking as many Allies with them as possible, and they only surrendered after American planes dropped atomic bombs on Hiroshima and Nagasaki, resulting in gruesome death and injury for tens of thousands. A total of forty-five million people died during the war, causing many to reframe their ideas about hell. Perhaps, they thought, hell was in the horror of what people like Elie Wiesel had experienced, a young teenager who was loaded into a death train along with his family and taken to Auschwitz to die. As for hell being the absence of God, some asked where God was in all that suffering. "Mac" McCarty recalls, "At the end of the War we liberated Mauthausen Concentration Camp in Austria. I don't mean to be overdramatic, but what I saw there made me doubt the existence of God for awhile. We stayed there about five weeks burying the dead." [25]

Maybe, some considered, the old teachings about heaven and hell should be recast in the light of this new and terrible experience. Maybe hell was really about babies being tossed into ovens and people digging their own graves, then getting mowed down with machine guns. Maybe hell was being incinerated by an atom bomb or tortured by Japanese soldiers until you pleaded for death. Maybe hell was a place after all, and that place was earth.

14

THE POST-WAR ERA:

ANXIETY AND

ASSURANCE

I n the fall of 1949, a young Baptist preacher from North Carolina told a Los Angeles audience that unless they repented of their sins, they were going to hell. He was scheduled to speak for three weeks, but the people were so spiritually hungry that the "crusade" extended to eight. Day after day he presented the gospel's compelling message to be born again, and thousands accepted Jesus Christ as their personal savior. Another evangelist took the preacher aside and accused him of setting back their cause by a hundred years. Billy Graham responded that he had hoped to set it back nearly two *thousand* years, to the time when it was said of the first Christians, "they turned the world upside down."

That first of Graham's evangelistic crusades catapulted him to national attention with feature stories in many newspapers, and the cover of *Time* magazine a few years later. He received numerous offers to promote himself, including a $5 million television contract from NBC to host his own show. But he remained single-minded in his commitment to fulfill Jesus' "Great Commission" to take the gospel to the ends of the earth. Throughout the '50s Graham traveled to London, Australia, and the United States urging people to get right with God because a day of judgment was coming. Whether he was speaking in America's heartland or the heart of Manhattan, his pulpit-pounding, Bible-thumping message remained the same.

On October 15, 1958, Graham preached a sermon titled straightforwardly "Heaven or Hell" at the Charlotte, N.C., Coliseum. He made no allowances for those who said hell was the pain we caused ourselves, or that it was here on earth. He spelled out for his listeners the two possible destinations that await each person:

> You do not have to serve God if you do not want to do so. You do not have to go to church if you do not want to do so. You do not have to read your Bible if you do not want to do so. But God said if you choose to live that kind of life, if you choose to live apart from Christ, there is judgment and destruction and hell in the future. . . .

> I have studied this book for twenty years, and I have tried to get around it, and I cannot. I cannot study the teachings of Jesus without believing that men are lost. I only know hell is separation from God. I only know Jesus warned us in no uncertain terms against going to hell. And He used the most terrible language to describe it. I believe that one minute after death those outside of Christ will discover the horrible mistake they have made; and they will say, "My God, my God."

In order for people to gain heaven, Graham explained, the Bible says that they must put their faith in Jesus Christ. There is no other way to that wonderful place:

> The Bible says there will be joy in heaven when we all get there to be at Jesus' feet. What a glorious time it is going to be, of singing and shouting and praising God and glorifying Him forever. Such exquisite beauty, such magnificence, such splendor.

> You must receive Him. When you stand at the entrance of eternity, you're going to be asked for a passport. Everywhere I go in the world I have to carry a little green American passport. I have to pull it out, and I can't get into any country unless I've got that passport. You can't get into heaven unless your passport is in order, unless it has been stamped by Christ. Is your passport in order? Has it been stamped? I want to tell you, if I didn't know tonight that my sins were forgiven, if I didn't know I was in Christ, you couldn't drag me out of this coliseum until I had settled it.[1]

It is a testimony to the mood of the times and the activity of God in history that Graham's ancient formula for attaining salvation was accepted in America's post–World War II era that lasted from 1945 to roughly 1960. Although that time is remembered as affluent and innocent, it is important not to overgeneralize when so many were struggling to overcome poverty and racial prejudice. In addition, it was a time of significant anxiety. With their newly gained wealth, many Americans were on the move as never before, leaving old neighborhoods in favor of new, sometimes distant, suburbs and striving to keep up with the Joneses to attain the "American dream." This was also the inaugural age of the atom bomb and the Cold War when American schoolchildren learned to duck under their desks and cover their heads in case the Russians bombed us into submission, or oblivion. People were deeply concerned when the Soviets made it first into space, launching the satellite *Sputnik* in 1957, because they might be tempted to drop their atomic bombs on the United States from outer space. There were those who believed that Armageddon, the final battle of mankind, might be at hand.

During the early 1950s, there was also another war, in Korea, as the United States tried to keep the Communist North Koreans and their Chinese allies from taking over the southern part of that country. The Korean War claimed over thirty-three thousand American lives. Americans greatly feared communism because it promoted atheism and denied freedom of religion to those living in its shadow, or behind its "iron curtain," as Winston Churchill put it. Americans took it literally when Soviet Premier Nikita Khrushchev told a group of Western diplomats, "Whether you like it or not, history is on our side. We will bury you!"[2]

Hollywood played on the public's fears with movies such as *The Day the Earth Stood Still*, in which creatures from outer space or those mutated by atomic blasts threatened civilization. In such a climate, many Americans were ready to listen to messages of sin and salvation, heaven and hell, for the first time in decades. There was a resurgence of evangelical Christianity during that time, including the formation of parachurch organizations like Youth for Christ, the National Association of Evangelicals, the Billy Graham Evangelistic Association, and Campus Crusade for Christ. In 1956 *Christianity Today* first appeared, along with Bethany Fellowship, which would become a major leader in Christian publishing. Carl Stuart Hamblen, a "singing cowboy," came to Christ during the Los Angeles Billy Graham Crusade, then hosted a popular radio show, "The Cowboy Church of the Air." He was one of several Christians with television or radio programs.

All of these organizations and individuals upheld an orthodox Christian view of heaven and hell, and they received a serious hearing from the public during this most modern of periods in American history. Church membership also rose dramatically, by 400–700 percent for conservative and evangelical denominations in the two decades following World War II, while the mainline churches enjoyed a more modest increase of 75–90 percent.[3]

∽∽∽

During the post-war era, Americans in large numbers came to believe that in order to be truly religious, one had to be patriotic, and in order to be patriotic, one also had to be religious. The preferred religion was Protestantism, but Roman Catholics and Jews also made a strong showing. In 1954 when the phrase "under God" was added to the Pledge of Allegiance, President Eisenhower said, "Our government makes no sense unless it is founded on a deeply felt religious faith—and I don't care what it is."[4] In 1956 Congress adopted a new official motto for the country, "In God we trust." In order to capitalize on this religious mood and to win public support at a time when several filmmakers and stars were under scrutiny for being possible Communist sympathizers, Hollywood trotted out a number of faith-based films. They included epics like *Ben Hur*, *The Ten Commandments*, *The Robe*, *Barabbas*, and *Demetrius and the Gladiators*.

Books with religious themes topped the best-seller lists throughout the '50s, among them Billy Graham's *Peace With God* and *The Secret of Happiness.* Along with Graham, another religious "star" rose, the Roman Catholic priest Fulton J. Sheen, who helped bring such celebrities as Clare Boothe Luce, Heywood Broun, and Henry Ford II into the Christian fold. His *Peace of Soul* appeared in 1949, accompanied by his radio program "The Catholic Hour" that boasted an audience of four million listeners. His television show drew roughly thirty million viewers in spite of running opposite the wildly popular Milton Berle program. Berle once quipped about Sheen, "He uses old material, too."[5] On a memorable telecast in February 1953, Sheen gave a dramatic reading of the funeral scene from *Julius Caesar*, but instead of the names Caesar, Mark Antony, Brutus, and Cassius, he substituted Joseph Stalin and other Soviet leaders' names. He concluded, "Stalin must one day meet his judgment." Premier Stalin died on March 5.[6]

Like Graham, Fulton Sheen believed in sin and salvation, heaven and hell, having been raised on the traditional Catholic catechism. Thomas Reeves says:

> The necessity of evangelism . . . was pounded into the minds and hearts of catechumens and seminarians. Fulton had heard the message from infancy . . . every soul lost to the Church might well be lost forever. All earthly events existed in the shadow of that moment described in Matthew 25, when Jesus Christ would return and divide the sheep from the goats, the faithful from the unbelieving, sending some to everlasting bliss and others to eternal fire and pain. What could be of more importance than eternity? Every priest, indeed every Christian, had the obligation to save souls. Some, like Fulton, took the duty with high seriousness.[7]

Sheen preached that unless a person received Christ, he would spend the afterlife in anguish. He warned those, especially among the theologians, who tried to sidestep issues of salvation, heaven, hell, and the devil, saying, "The demonic is always most powerful when he is denied."[8]

ᏜᎤᎤᏛ

Another popular Christian writer of the post-war period was Catherine Marshall. Her husband, Peter, was the pastor of Washington's New York Avenue Presbyterian Church and the Senate Chaplain when he died suddenly in 1949 at 46. Her collection of his sermons, *Mr. Jones, Meet the Master*, became an enormous best seller, and she went on to write his biography, *A Man Called Peter*, which has sold over four million copies since it first appeared, and became a major motion picture. Her frank style invited intimacy with God and the assurance that in Him, people could overcome any adversity. A particularly moving scene in both the biography and the movie had her saying good-bye to Peter after his second heart attack as he was carried to an ambulance. Her words, "See you, darling, see you in the morning," were prophetic; he died shortly afterward at the hospital. However, her faith assured her, and all those who read the words in print or heard them on the screen, that she would see Peter on the Other Side.

A British writer who had a significant impact on American religion in that era was C. S. Lewis, professor of English Literature at Oxford and Cambridge universities. An avowed atheist for much of his youth, Lewis became a devout Anglican and an apologist for orthodox Christianity in an environment deeply hostile to it. Along with his friend J. R. R. Tolkien, Lewis employed his rich imagination and intellect to explain ancient truths to modern readers. Perhaps one of his powerful appeals to American evangelicals was the way he demonstrated that people don't have to check their brains at the door to become believers. Says Joseph Loconte, "While Oxford agnostics howled, Lewis gave BBC talks on theology that were a national sensation. Even his beloved children's stories, *The Chronicles of Narnia*, ring with biblical themes of sin and redemption. No one did more to make 'the repellent doctrines' of Christianity plausible to modern ears."[9] Lewis believed that it was up to each individual to determine what his or her final destiny would be, whether it would be oriented toward the self, or toward God. "Sin is ultimately the choosing of self over God. Damnation and Hell are receiving that choice of self over God forever. . . . Hell is the final inability to choose anything but the self."[10]

Another popular writer and radio preacher was the brilliant Donald Grey Barnhouse, pastor of Philadelphia's Tenth Presbyterian Church and founder of *Eternity* magazine. Like the intellectual Lewis, he didn't shy away from confronting people with their need for salvation. According to one story, Barnhouse once met a young man who had grown up in a completely atheistic environment and who felt headed for an emotional collapse. He told the pastor that when he was 17, his father died, but there had been no service for him. At the grave, a lawyer read a statement from the father that said,

> I wish to testify that I have lived my life without religion and without any superstitious belief in any God or devil, and I wish it known that I have died as any animal, for we are all part of the evolutionary process, and when death comes we die like any other animal. It is in this belief that I have lived and died.[11]

"The others walked away," the young man recalled, "and I was left standing there alone." Barnhouse told him in no uncertain terms that he had to "take sides with God against his father." The fellow jumped up and exclaimed, "Do you realize what you are asking me to do? You are asking me to say my father is in hell." Even so, Barnhouse wouldn't let up. "If he is, it will not help the situation you are in. You must take sides with God against your father and say, 'God, my father deserved to go to hell, and I deserve to go to hell.'" The young man fell to his knees sobbing and confessed his belief in God, and in His Son, Jesus Christ.

∽•∽

In 1950s America other religious leaders appeared on the scene, writing and preaching to great public acclaim, including those who sometimes took a less confrontational, orthodox, or sometimes even Christian view of sin and salvation. Rabbi Joshua Loth Liebman was an accomplished young man who graduated from college at the age of nineteen. He became a lecturer at Hebrew Union College in Cincinnati, then served a synagogue in Boston. Liebman often preached on the radio, and his 1946 book *Peace of Mind* was another religious best seller. One of the first "self-help" books, it stressed the benevolence of God and His desire to give individuals peace and happiness, which was a major theme at that time.

In 1952 Norman Vincent Peale became famous after the publication of *The Power of Positive Thinking*. It sold in the millions, was translated into thirty-three languages, and spent three years on the *New York Times* best-seller list. In it he encouraged people to find peace and self-fulfillment by learning to utilize God's power in their lives, by practicing positive thinking and avoiding negativity. The pastor of New York's Marble Collegiate Church and founder of *Guideposts* magazine, he disliked speaking about hell because it was negative. The Rev. Walter Martin once wrote about a meeting that took place in those days between his mentor, Donald Grey Barnhouse, and Peale. The latter asked Barnhouse to share his thoughts about positive thinking, and Barnhouse responded:

> "You have forgotten the most important thing. Before anyone can think positively, they must think negatively."

> "What do you mean by that?" Peale asked.

> "Look," said Barnhouse, "I am a sinner. Negative or positive?"

> "Negative."

> "I am a lost sinner. Negative or positive?"

> "Negative."

> "I am going to eternal judgment. Negative or positive."

> "Negative."

Dr. Barnhouse smiled, "Those are three negative propositions, without which, you cannot think positively. 'Believe on the Lord Jesus Christ and thou shalt be saved' (Acts 16:31). But if you don't think the first three, you'll never get to the fourth."

"I never thought of it quite that way before," answered Dr. Peale, rather disturbed.

"You must write a new book," said Dr. Barnhouse, "The Power of Negative Thinking."

"I can't do that; it would ruin me!"

"Get out the truth," said Barnhouse. "The Lord will take care of it."[12]

In his 1958 book *The Surge of Piety in America: An Appraisal*, Roy Eckhardt referred to Peale as "the high priest of the cult of reassurance."[13] He said that Peale was correct to emphasize that believers could connect with God's power in their lives, but that Peale was making God seem like "an automatically operating machine . . . and more the servant of man than the sovereign creator and judge of all things."[14] Although others said they found "Paul appealing and Peale appalling," it cannot be denied that Peale's philosophy affected anxious Americans so deeply that it is difficult to overestimate his importance.

∽o∾

In the post-war period, the mass media's influence increased significantly. While Hollywood turned out some thoughtful, if not entirely accurate, biblical epics and faith-oriented films, it is interesting to note the way in which movie makers, who had the public's overall trust, handled the afterlife. At times, as with *A Man Called Peter*, its treatment was tender and winsome—"See you darling, see you in the morning." There was also the scene in *The Inn of the Sixth Happiness* in which missionary Gladys Aylward was helping a large number of Chinese children dodge invading Japanese soldiers after her helper, Lee, died while acting as a decoy. She reassured the weary and frightened children, "You must think of how happy our good friend Lee, who is in heaven, would be for us." It is interesting that while she said Lee had gone to be with God, she did not say that he was "up there looking down on us."

There were also some whimsical, odd, even secular portrayals of the afterlife. One of the former was *It's a Wonderful Life*, Frank Capra's perennial Christmas classic about depressed George Bailey who was thwarted and frustrated at every turn. When his family's and friends' prayers reached heaven, the head angel sent Clarence Oddbody, an "Angel Second Class" eager to get his wings, to Bailey's rescue. That film advanced the biblically untenable, though increasingly popular, view that when people die, they become angels who can revisit earth to assist the living.

In the 1953 musical *The Band Wagon*, there was an over-the-top Faustian scene from hell complete with copious flames and moaning and groaning. Similarly comic was a number from *Guys and Dolls* (1955) in which gambler Nicely Nicely sang about going to heaven in a boat, although it was clear that he should have been going to the other place.

An oddly secular view of life after death appeared in the 1947 film *The Ghost and Mrs. Muir* in which a widow, Lucy Muir, and her daughter went to live in a seaside cottage haunted by its former owner, a dead sea captain. When Lucy refused to be frightened away, he formed a bond with her. After she eventually developed a relationship with a living man, the captain eased himself out of her life. The fellow turned out to be a scoundrel, so Lucy went on with a quiet life in the cottage until she died years later. Then the captain ushered her into the hereafter. There was nothing even remotely faith-oriented in this movie, just the idea that people live on after they die, sometimes as restless ghosts until they solve a specific problem. This was a common view in that era among people without a firm foundation in Jesus Christ.

∽∘∾

Television became even more influential than the movies in the '50s, and most Americans innocently believed that if something was on TV, it had to be true. People stopped what they were doing each week to watch their favorite programs, especially *I Love Lucy*, and the Milton Berle and Ed Sullivan shows. Researchers discovered that teenagers spent more time in front of the TV than in school. John Garraty says, "The entertainment offered by most television stations was generally abominable; Newton Minow of the FCC called it a 'vast wasteland.'"[15] One of those shows, *Topper*, was inspired by a 1937 movie of the same name in which a straight-laced bank president and his wife bought a house that was haunted by its previous owners, as well as their deceased dog. Only Mr. Topper could see them. Like *The Ghost and Mrs. Muir*, it propped up the notion that people can become ghosts upon their deaths, haunting the living until they resolve their problems and go to heaven.

Rock and roll dominated popular music in the 1950s, and at least two songs in that genre provided unorthodox views of the hereafter. "Endless Sleep," recorded by Jody Reynolds in 1958, was banned by many radio stations because it dealt with suicide. After quarreling with her boyfriend, a girl tried to drown herself in the ocean, but he rescued her in time from death, or an "endless sleep." Much more popular was the 1960 hit "Teen Angel" by Mark Dinning in which a couple's car got stuck on a railroad track and the girl, after being saved from the wreck, ran back and was killed. Afterward, the boy found his high school ring in her hand and sang to her as a "teen angel," wondering if she could remain his true love if she was in heaven. Once again, there was the notion that dead humans became angels, as well as the unspoken assumption that, of course, the girl would be going to heaven.

∽o∽

In the first days of March 1953, official communiques announced to the Soviet people that their leader, Joseph Stalin, was gravely ill. After the third bulletin, Russian Orthodox priests and clergy from other churches held services in which they called for prayers for the avowed atheist. Rabbis also asked their people "to bless the man who had so recently set in motion the scourge of anti-Semitism."[16] Six hours later came the final declaration: "The heart of . . . Joseph Vissarionovich Stalin has stopped beating. . . . Long live the great and all-conquering teachings of Marx, Engels, Lenin and Stalin! Long live our heroic Soviet people!"[17] Stalin's funeral was completely devoid of faith, centered on his achievements and the glories of the Communist Party. After several speakers gave their atheistic eulogies, the premier's body was taken to the official mausoleum. As *Time* magazine noted for its highly religious American audience:

> At the first stroke of noon by the Kremlin clock, a wave of sound—
> artillery salvos, clanging chimes, blasting factory whistles—rang across
> Soviet Russia and its satellites. Thus was the conqueror laid to rest—not
> with a prayer, but with whistle's scream and cannon's roar.[18]

When Stalin passed away, there was little guesswork for journalists about his ultimate destination, but they had a far trickier time when three beloved Americans died, none of whom had professed faith in Christ, except possibly for one. Instead of proclaiming that each of these men went to heaven, as reporters so often do today—if they even believe in such a place—that era's writers took a far more cautious tone. This was the case when the beloved genius Albert Einstein died in Princeton, New Jersey, on April 18, 1955. There was no funeral, his brain went to science, and his ashes were spread over a river. In its obituary, the *New York Times* seemed to offer hope for his soul to those who loved and admired Einstein by saying that he did, after all, believe in God, and even referred to the scientist as a mystic with deep thoughts about the Divine Being:

> While he did not believe in a formal, dogmatic religion, Dr. Einstein,
> like all true mystics, was of a deeply religious nature. He referred to it
> as the cosmic religion, which he defined as a seeking on the part of the
> individual who feels it "to experience the totality of existence as a unity
> full of significance."

> [Einstein said,] "I cannot imagine a God who rewards and punishes the objects of his creation, whose purposes are modeled after our own—a God, in short, who is but a reflection of human fraility. Neither can I believe that the individual survives the death of his body, although feeble souls harbor such thoughts through fear or ridiculous egotism. It is enough for me to contemplate the mystery of conscious life perpetuating itself through all eternity, to reflect upon the marvelous structure of the universe which we can dimly perceive, and to try humbly to comprehend even an infinitesimal part of the intelligence manifested in nature.
>
> "My religion consists of a humble admiration of the illimitable superior spirit who reveals himself in the slight details we are able to perceive with our frail and feeble minds. That deeply emotional conviction of the presence of a superior reasoning power, which is revealed in the incomprehensible universe, forms my idea of God."[19]

When James Dean showed off his new Porsche 550 Spyder to fellow actor Alec Guinness on September 23, 1955, Guinness told him that the vehicle looked "sinister." He warned, "If you get in that car, you will be found dead in it by this time next week."[20] Exactly a week later, Dean died in a head-on collision with an unsuspecting college student, who survived. Although Dean was raised in the Quaker tradition and was befriended by a Methodist pastor as a teenager, he left them in favor of a fast, brooding lifestyle that included sexual experimentation, booze, and fast cars. After seeing his film *East of Eden*, critic Pauline Kael gushed, "Look at all that beautiful desperation."[21] Those who wrote about the twenty-four-year-old actor's untimely death would note wistfully that his memorial service was held at his childhood church, the Back Creek Friends Meeting in Fairmount, Indiana, with a burial in the adjoining cemetery. It seemed too depressing to think of darker possibilities.

There seemed to be more hope for singer Buddy Holly, who along with two other entertainers, perished in a plane crash during a snowstorm in February 1959. The twenty-two-year-old was raised in a strict fundamentalist Baptist church and, at fourteen, had made a profession of faith and been baptized. Nevertheless, he became a wild young man who smoked, drank, shoplifted, and slept around. Larry Holly, his older brother, claimed that Buddy told him that he planned to leave the music industry after he made enough money to get out of debt and live more righteously.[22] He ran out of time. Larry Holly believed that Buddy was saved, though backslidden at the time of his death.

It had been far easier for journalists to speculate about the eternal destination of five young missionaries to Ecuador. Nate Saint, Jim Elliot, Ed McCully, Peter Fleming, and Roger Youderian, all in their prime and living for Jesus, set out to win Ecudaor's Auca Indians for the Lord. On January 8, 1956, they encountered several tribesmen on a beach. The Auca men speared the five missionaries to death. The story of their martyrdom made headlines in the United States, including a ten-page story in *Life* magazine and a *Reader's Digest* feature. Their examples sparked a deepened interest in missions among countless young Americans who wanted to usher people into the heaven that those men entered when they died.

∽o∽

The post-war era was the last time that Christianity was mostly at peace with mainstream American culture, when it still set the tone and stood as a trusted authority for life and death—not *the* authority as it had been in other centuries, but an essential one nonetheless. The revival that helped bring this about began to wane around 1960, and in the next ten years a rebellious spirit lingering under the surface of society would break out in ways that few could have imagined.

15

EVE OF
DESTRUCTION?

O n January 21, 1961, John F. Kennedy gave notice in his inaugural speech that things were about to change in America. "Let the word go forth from this time and place," he said, "to friend and foe alike, that the torch has been passed to a new generation of Americans—born in this century, tempered by war, disciplined by a hard and bitter peace, proud of our ancient heritage."[1] When Kennedy ran for president, some Americans worried that as a Catholic, he would let the pope dictate national policy. They need not have been concerned, since the Massachusetts senator was not known for deep piety. As his presidency played itself out, the national media cast it in romantic terms. JFK was the youngest elected president in U.S. history, and his even younger wife, Jacqueline, personified elegance while their two children charmed the nation. Brilliant cabinet members offered what they believed was a new and better way of approaching challenges. JFK found the romanticizing amusing, but he allowed the perception to stick because it was favorable.

John Kennedy was essentially a pragmatist with a deep commitment to secularism. In previous generations, American leaders ruled from a moral foundation based on Christian principles, even if they didn't always follow them. Kennedy and his circle, however, followed the philosophy popularized by John Dewey and William James. According to pragmatism, truth is relative and must be decided by each person on the basis of its usefulness. James once said, "In this real world of sweat and dirt, it seems to me that when a view of things is 'noble,' that it ought to count as a presumption against its truth."[2] Pragmatists also thought of society as a machine; if its parts were understood well enough, it could be made to work. The national mood was such that during Kennedy's administration the Supreme Court ruled sponsored Bible readings and prayers were unconstitutional in public schools.

Kennedy was not a believer in the Christian doctrine of original sin or, therefore, the need for divine redemption. He thought most problems could be solved using reason and that people were motivated more by good will based on common sense and the common good than on having to answer to Almighty God. He didn't seem to understand that many issues are largely morally or spiritually driven. It became much more apparent, however, when various Southern public officials turned attack dogs and fire hoses on peaceful civil rights demonstrators, including children, and when activist Medgar Evers was gunned down in the driveway of his Mississippi home. Filled with the spirit of violence, the perpetrators could not be reasoned with.

An especially tragic example of this took place in September 1963, when four little girls died in the bombing of their Birmingham, Alabama, church. Martin Luther King Jr., also the target of threats, understood the moral and spiritual dimensions of civil rights. He cast their deaths in a Christian light and appealed to the good will of Americans to change the great evil that was befalling the country. It was enough to make Kennedy think twice about always being pragmatic. In his funeral sermon for three of the girls, King spoke of how they had died nobly, that they were "the martyred heroes of a holy crusade for freedom and human dignity."[3] Then he said, "In a real sense they have something to say to each of us in their death." Rather than, "They are in heaven looking down on us," he spoke in terms of their deaths being a call to action for the fearful, the complacent, and the hypocritical. Then he appealed to

Christianity's affirmation that death is not the end. Death is not a period that ends the great sentence of life, but a comma that punctuates it to more lofty significance. Death is not a blind alley that leads the human race into a state of nothingness, but an open door which leads man into life eternal. Let this daring faith, this great invincible surmise, be your sustaining power during these trying days.[4]

∽๐๛

There would be a great deal more death and fear in the coming days and years of that decade. Later in the fall of 1963, death inflicted an even deeper wound. On November 22, while President Kennedy rode in a motorcade through Dallas, Texas, a sniper shot and killed him, unleashing what Sydney Ahlstrom called "a concert of grief such as human technology could never before have made possible."[5] It was the first time that a U.S. president had been assassinated since McKinley sixty-two years earlier, and the way that the press, officials, and the public responded were very different. No one in 1901, for example, was subjected to a relentless replay of the shooting on television, or the arrest, then murder, of the accused assassin afterward, along with coverage of the funeral and procession to Arlington National Cemetery with all of its terrible solemnity. Many Americans did little else in those days besides watch TV coverage. Also different was the way in which Kennedy was remembered and mourned. President McKinley, an ardent Christian, was hailed as a son of the true faith who had gone on to his heavenly reward; if Americans were wise, they would follow his example. The Kennedy funeral revealed a paradigm shift in American thinking about death. While Kennedy was mourned as a Roman Catholic with a requiem Mass, there was a curious blending of the sacred and the secular in tributes made about him. At the Capitol Rotunda, Supreme Court Chief Justice Earl Warren said that Americans were a better people because of the quality of his leadership:

> Our Nation is bereaved. The whole world is poorer because of his loss.
> But we can all be better Americans because John Fitzgerald Kennedy

has passed our way, because he has been our chosen leader at a time in history when his character, his vision, and his quiet courage have enabled him to chart a course for us—a safe course for us, through the shoals of treacherous seas that encompass the world.

And now that he is relieved of the almost superhuman burden we imposed on him, may he rest in peace.[6]

Similarly, Senate Majority Leader Mike Mansfield painted a romantic portrait of a fallen hero whom Americans would do best to emulate in the coming years, although not because of his godliness. Still, it would take God's help for the public to be more like JFK:

A piece of each of us died at that moment. Yet, in death he gave of himself to us. He gave us of a good heart from which the laughter came. He gave us of a profound wit, from which a great leadership emerged. He gave us of a kindness and a strength fused into a human courage to seek peace without fear.

He gave us of his love that we, too, in turn, might give. He gave that we might give of ourselves, that we might give to one another until there would be no room, no room at all, for the bigotry, the hatred, prejudice, and the arrogance which converged in that moment of horror to strike him down.

In leaving us—these gifts, John Fitzgerald Kennedy, President of the United States, leaves with us. Will we take them, Mr. President? Will we have, now, the sense and the responsibility and the courage to take them?

I pray to God that we shall and under God we will.[7]

John W. McCormack, Speaker of the House, gave a related message commenting on Kennedy's place in history, and not his place in heaven:

Now that our great leader has been taken from us in a cruel death, we are bound to feel shattered and helpless in the face of our loss. This is but natural, but as the first bitter pangs of our incredulous grief begin to pass we must thank God that we were privileged, however briefly, to have had this great man for our President. For he has now taken his place among the great figures of world history.

While this is an occasion of deep sorrow it should be also one of dedication. We must have the determination to unite and carry on the spirit of John Fitzgerald Kennedy for a strengthened America and a future world of peace.[8]

Even at the Mass, the emphasis was on Kennedy the man, rather than Kennedy the man of God, and instead of giving a sermon, the Most Reverend Philip M. Hannan read selections from Kennedy's speeches and prose. A few of those included biblical references. On the way to Washington aboard Air Force One, Lyndon Johnson was hastily sworn in, but no one could find a Bible for him to place his hand on while taking the Oath of Office. Someone finally located a Catholic missal in JFK's desk, and it was pressed into service. As Kennedy had said at his inauguration, the torch had passed to a new generation of leaders, secular men who preferred reason to religion.

When other public notables died during the 1960s, media observers seemed reluctant even to mention heaven. Perhaps they were no longer sure about what it was or who went there. Maybe it seemed too simple an idea to those who lived outside of the orthodox Christian tradition. When Eleanor Roosevelt, Winston Churchill, and Marilyn Monroe passed away, there were references to Christian services in papers and magazines, but little in the way of what might come next for them. In his eulogy to Monroe, actor and director Lee Strasberg gave no reassurance, just a reference to the universality of death:

Now it is at an end. I hope her death will stir sympathy and understanding for a sensitive artist and a woman who brought joy and pleasure to the world.

I cannot say goodby. Marilyn never liked goodbys, but in the peculiar way she had of turning things around so that they faced reality—I will say au revoir. For the country to which she has gone, we must all someday visit.[9]

∽o∾

In the 1960s TV, radio, and the print media all assigned major status to rock and roll bands that helped create a "counterculture," one that
went against Judeo-Christian thought. Chief among these was the Beatles, who captured America's affection in the months just after Kennedy's
assassination. They might have worn suits and sung innocently about
wanting to hold a girl's hand, but their long hair—by that day's standards—and irreverence made many parents wary, even if the respected
Ed Sullivan had given them his secular blessing. It was, after all, the Beatles who paved the way for the frank worldliness of the Rolling Stones and
other iconoclastic bands. (In their own appearance on the *Ed Sullivan
Show*, the host made them change the provocative lyrics of "Let's Spend
the Night Together" to "spend some time together.") In a March 1966,
interview, John Lennon remarked, "Christianity will go. . . . It will vanish
and shrink. I needn't argue with that; I'm right and I will be proved right.
We're more popular than Jesus now; I don't know which will go first—
rock-and-roll or Christianity. Jesus was all right, but his disciples were
thick and ordinary. It's them twisting it that ruins it for me."[10] Lennon
later apologized, saying he didn't mean to imply that the Beatles were
better than Jesus or that Lennon was anti-God or anti-Christian, just
that they had eclipsed Jesus in terms of popularity. Although some parents and radio stations banned their music—for a while—and some teens
burned their records, there was something eerily correct about Lennon's
feckless comment. At least as far as the media and its hold on popular
culture were concerned, Jesus had been replaced by those who did not
see the world, or the world to come, from His point of view.

Throughout the '60s, Americans listened to and watched a steady
diet of entertainment that chipped away at the foundations of Christian
belief. When the Beatles cozied up to the Maharishi Mahesh Yogi, many
Americans became interested in Hinduism, Transcendental Meditation,
and Yoga. They began to take seriously the teachings of reincarnation,

preferring the thought of returning to the world after death in a different form until they got it right to the torments of hell or heavenly harp-playing. In the 1965 sitcom *My Mother the Car*, a beat-up old vehicle was the reincarnation of a man's mother, and several other programs popularized ghosts, witches, demons, and vampires, including *The Ghost and Mrs. Muir*, *Bewitched*, and *Dark Shadows*. The Rolling Stones came out with a song called "Sympathy for the Devil" and an album, *Their Satanic Majesties Request*. It matters less that they portrayed the Devil as the horror that he is than that they were bold enough to draw that kind of guileless attention to him.

Sex, drugs, and rock and roll prevailed in the latter part of the decade for heralds of pop culture. People spoke of the new birth control pill, the push for legalized abortion, and women's rights in terms of a "new morality," which was actually quite old. Without concern for a final judgement before a holy God, most people chose to do their own thing, including having sex outside of marriage.

～∽～

In Barry McGuire's haunting hit song "Eve of Destruction," he sang of the world dying at the push of a button that would begin a nuclear war and how because of that threat, and the violence exploding everywhere he looked, the world was facing its own demise. In 1968, it appeared that his prophecy might be coming true, that, indeed, all hell was breaking loose—beginning in Vietnam where nearly sixty thousand Americans would die over the course of the conflict. It was a nightmare for those who fought in that war, including Charles McHugh, a twenty-one-year-old Marine from the Philadelphia area. On the morning of January 30, 1968, he and his buddies awakened to the "Tet Offensive." It was the largest military operation at that point in the war, and McHugh faced constant danger and possible death. In that environment, his Roman Catholic faith and belief in heaven helped him cope. "You think about death all the time" in a situation like that, he said. "I feared for my life all the time, cause you saw it all the time. When I was in danger, I would pray." Sometimes, he says, his prayers were the more formal ones of his Catholic upbringing, but when death seemed especially near, they would be more like "God, help me!" He wasn't afraid of going to hell because "at that young age, I thought I was a good person, that I hadn't lived long enough to do anything really bad. If I died, I hoped I'd go to heaven, but I thought I was in hell sometimes. As for purgatory, well, that I could take. It was death I was afraid of, not hell."[11] His perspective was a common one, typical of American fighting men since the world wars.

As the hostilities intensified in the spring of 1968, so did the efforts of antiwar protestors back home, mostly college students, who sometimes burned draft cards and/or fled to Canada to avoid the draft. Some entered seminary and the ministry to stay out of the fighting. There was also growing unrest within the civil rights movement as blacks like Bobby Seale, Huey Newton, and Eldridge Cleaver charged that Martin Luther King Jr.'s nonviolent movement wasn't getting them anywhere, that it was time to use bloodshed to achieve their goals.

While trying to hold the black coalition together, King lent his support to a group of striking sanitation workers in Memphis, Tennessee, in early April. While he spoke of attaining full equality with whites, there was also a ring of mortality in his biblically laced words to the pickets:

> Well, I don't know what will happen now. We've got some difficult days ahead. But it doesn't matter with me now. Because I've been to the mountaintop. And I don't mind. Like anybody, I would like to live a long life. Longevity has its place. But I'm not concerned about that now. I just want to do God's will. And He's allowed me to go up to the mountain. And I've looked over. And I've seen the promised land. I may not get there with you. But I want you to know tonight, that we, as a people, will get to the promised land. And I'm happy, tonight. I'm not worried about anything. I'm not fearing any man. Mine eyes have seen the glory of the coming of the Lord.[12]

Just after six o'clock the following evening, an assassin shot King while the civil rights leader stood on his motel balcony. When Senator Robert F. Kennedy, who was campaigning for the Democratic nomination for the presidency, heard the news, he went to a scheduled stop at an Indianapolis ghetto and told the people what had happened. As the crowd stood in shock, Kennedy combined an appeal to prayer with a quote from a Greek philosopher: "He who learns must suffer. Even in our sleep, pain which cannot forget falls drop by drop upon the heart until, in our own despair, and against our will, comes wisdom by the awful grace of God."[13] As in the case with the more secular John Kennedy, the various tributes to King didn't mention heaven but that he had been a prophet like Amos and Micah, Jesus, and Martin Luther. At King's funeral, his friend Benjamin Mays said, "Martin Luther King Jr.'s unfinished work on earth must truly be our own."[14] Especially for a minister of the gospel, the accolades weren't focused on heaven as they surely would have been in previous decades.

Many riots broke out in America's inner cities during the next days and weeks as distressed and grieving residents vented their rage. With the war in Vietnam reaching new levels of death and destruction, it seemed like violence was engulfing the country. It was about to get worse.

Robert Kennedy won a critical primary in California on June 4, and right around midnight addressed a crowd of supporters in the ballroom of Los Angeles's Ambassador Hotel. After finishing his speech, he took a shortcut through the kitchen where shots rang out, and he went down, blood oozing from a head wound. A priest who was nearby rushed over to Kennedy and put a rosary into his hands while someone shoved the cleric yelling, "He doesn't need a priest, for God's sake, he needs a doctor!" Another symbol of authority, a police officer, received similar treatment when he came in bearing a shotgun. "We don't need guns! We need a doctor!"[15] When Cardinal Cushing, a Kennedy family friend, heard about the shooting, he offered little comfort based on faith: "All I can say is, good Lord, what is this all about? We could continue our prayers that it would never happen again, but we did that before."[16]

Robert's brother, Senator Edward Kennedy, gave the eulogy at the funeral, his remarks reflecting a blend of John Kennedy's pragmatism and Robert Kennedy's idealism. He didn't say anything about the rewards of RFK's faith:

> "Our future may lie beyond our vision, but it is not completely beyond our control. It is the shaping impulse of America that neither fate nor nature nor the irresistible tides of history, but the work of our own hands, matched to reason and principle, that will determine our destiny. There is pride in that, even arrogance, but there is also experience and truth. In any event, it is the only way we can live."

> This is the way he lived. My brother need not be idealized, or enlarged in death beyond what he was in life, to be remembered simply as a good and decent man, who saw wrong and tried to right it, saw suffering and tried to heal it, saw war and tried to stop it.

> Those of us who loved him and who take him to his rest today, pray that what he was to us and what he wished for others will some day come to pass for all the world.

> As he said many times, in many parts of this nation, to those he touched and who sought to touch him:

> "Some men see things as they are and say why. I dream things that never were and say why not."[17]

∽○∽

During that cruel and convulsive time in American history, Blood, Sweat, and Tears sang about swearing there was no heaven and praying there was no hell, and John Lennon invited people to imagine there was neither heaven nor hell, just living in peace for each day. Back then when he came to Christ, John Karraker wasn't thinking as much about heaven and hell as he was feeling afraid about the future. That was in December of 1970, the same year Hal Lindsey's blockbuster *The Late, Great Planet*

Earth came out. Based on biblical prophecies about the end times, Lindsey used current events to demonstrate his belief that the world was on the edge of the last days while urging people to get right with God before it was too late. One of the things that drew Karraker, now director of theological development for Student Venture, to faith in Jesus Christ was prophecy. He says, "The suggestion that the world was going to end and that the Bible revealed how really grabbed me. Hal Lindsey's [book] was very scary to me . . . the idea that life was going to end and then came judgement was compelling."[18]

In the late '60s and early '70s, God was breaking through the clamor in some intriguing ways. It might have seemed that young people had given up on traditional expressions of Christianity, but in fact, they were still asking questions about Jesus. The highly successful rock opera *Jesus Christ Superstar* took a modern look at the old, old story, as well as the musical *Godspell*. One interviewer who covered a Pittsburgh production of *Superstar* in 1971 said he thought that Jesus now seemed bigger than the Beatles.[19] The Jesus in that play wasn't anywhere near an orthodox portrayal, but there was no doubt that young people were flocking to the real deal. Known as "Jesus People" and "Jesus Freaks," a mini-culture grew up around these new-style hippies. The pop music charts contained hits about the Lord such as "Day by Day," "Put Your Hand in the Hand," and "Jesus Is Just Alright." Barry "Eve of Destruction" McGuire, who had performed in the lascivious Broadway musical *Hair*, became "born again." He went on to launch the contemporary Christian music genre.

Even those who didn't know Christ were taken with Him. One memorable 1970 hit song was Norman Greenbaum's "Spirit in the Sky" about where he would be going when he died. Greenbaum was a Jew who felt inspired to do the song after seeing Porter Wagoner, a Gospel-singing country artist, on TV. Regarding his own convictions about the afterlife, Greenbaum says, "I believe in an energy force, sort of unexplainable since I'm not dead." He meant not only to entertain with the song, but also to be "an inspiration never to lose faith."[20] It was still a matter of

some importance among the young to know where they were going to
end up after this life ended.

In addition to the growing popularity of Bible prophecy and the
Jesus Movement, the charismatic renewal got underway beginning on
the West Coast, mostly associated with the ministry of Dennis Bennett,
an Episcopal priest. Unlike the Azusa Street and subsequent revivals at
the beginning of the century, this one deeply touched Christians within
mainline churches and Roman Catholicism.

While radical college students were disrupting life in U.S. cities,
God Himself interrupted the easy pace at a small Methodist school in
Kentucky. On a cold and windy February day in 1970, one thousand
Asburians gathered for 10:00 a.m. chapel where the dean had been
scheduled to preach. At the last minute, however, he felt compelled to
let a student give a testimony about what God was doing in his life. Then
the dean invited a few others to do the same. As the students spoke, a
powerful awareness of God's presence filled the auditorium, and when
the bell rang for classes to begin, it went unheeded as students began,
one after another, to confess their sins. The rest of the day's classes were
cancelled, and people lost track of time, forgetting even to eat and sleep.
On February 10, a full week later, classes were resumed, but the chapel
remained open for prayer, and nightly meetings continued. The effects
of the revival spread far beyond Asbury, wherever teams of students took
the story to other campuses.

One Asbury coed took a bus to Cincinnati, and her seat partner asked
why she was reading the Bible. She told him that she loved God's Word,
then shared how he could know Christ. The man asked her to tell this to
his friend in another seat, so the men switched seats, and the girl repeated
her story. At that point, an elderly man sitting in front of her asked if she
would speak up because he hadn't been able to understand every word.
A woman sitting across from the Asburian wanted to hear more, too. The
coed rose, went to the front of the bus, and gave her testimony to everyone. When they arrived in Cincinnati, the driver turned around and

asked her, "Do you have anything more to say?" She responded, "All I want to say is hallelujah!"

Don Daniels wrote in the *Wheeling News Register* that what happened at Asbury told him that "there remains on the nation's campuses a hard core sense of morality, and that in the final analysis the mark on history will be written by the people who spurn the podium of militant dissent in favor of a quiet place to talk with God "[21] Sydney Ahlstrom adds,

> In a time of change and confusion, some Americans wondered whether the old foundations still stood. There was still a majority consensus about traditional Christian beliefs, but it was with a diminishing degree of certainty and frequently came mixed up with other influences. The 60s were a time when people began to marry outside of their faith in increasing numbers, when divorce rose to new levels, and "radically revised foundations of belief were being laid."[22]

However, in the midst of upheaval, Ahlstrom says, "Most adult Americans . . . still held . . . to the religious convictions of earlier years."[23]

Overall, however, the American church was more concerned with contemporary issues than those related to heaven and hell. With the "gates of hell" pressing against the church, the threats of nuclear annihilation and societal disintegration seemed far more real than the more obscure and less immediate threat of hell. God was far from dead, and many Americans were still listening to His voice, but what of those who refused? Very few were sure, or could agree, about that.

16

ANYTHING
GOES

H e won the presidency in 1968 after promising a return to law and order in America's streets and an end to the Vietnam War. Just after his second inauguration, Richard Nixon signed the Paris Peace Accord, on January 27, 1973. It was an eventful week; former President Lyndon B. Johnson's weakened heart beat for the last time on January 22. The man who during his last years in the White House had endured a constant barrage of young people shouting at him, "Hey, hey, LBJ, how many kids did you kill today?" died at sixty-four at his Texas ranch. He looked twenty years older. Ex-governor of Texas John Connally spoke at the burial in the Johnson family cemetery near the Pedernales River. He said, "Along this stream and under these trees he loved, he will now rest. He first saw light here. He last felt life here. May he now find peace here."[1]

It seemed for a moment that a frenzied era had ended, that it was time to get on with a new decade, but there was one more significant commotion for Americans to endure before the spirit of the '60s would loosen its tenacious grip. It wasn't until after Nixon's reelection that the bungled Watergate burglary began to touch him personally. One by one, prosecutors picked off some of the president's closest associates, including his chief counsel, Charles Colson, and the man who headed up the Committee to Reelect the President, Jeb Stuart Magruder. Throughout the ordeal, Nixon maintained his innocence, declaring that he was not "a crook." By the summer of 1974, however, no one really believed that he hadn't been involved in the cover-up of the break-in at the Democratic Committee Headquarters. Rather than face impeachment, Nixon resigned, the first time an American president had stepped down while in office. On August 9, 1974, the new and unelected president, Gerald R. Ford, took the oath of office in a subdued ceremony. In his first speech to the nation he stated, "My fellow Americans, our long national nightmare is over." It may truly be said that at that moment the '60s had ended, and the 1970s began.

∽o∽

The country awakened to something along the lines of a national orgy as many Americans cast off traditional morality like last season's wardrobe and began doing exactly as they pleased. There was for such people a genuine lack of concern for consequences, either present or future. If most Americans in the 1960s still based their lives at least to some degree on Judeo-Christian morality, that support crumbled in the '70s. That decade, and the next, witnessed a paradigm shift in worldview from a specific moral base to a pluralistic one, as well as increasing decadence, and a crisis of authority. For example, when the Roman Catholic Church said "no" to artificial birth control, most of its American members said, "Forget it!" With abortion becoming legal in 1973, women were able to become more sexually active outside of marriage, apart from the usual consequences. In the "me" decade, advertisers urged people to have it their way and to indulge themselves because they were worth it. Instead of seeing themselves as sinners in need of God's grace, many Americans thought of themselves along the lines of a best-selling book, *I'm Okay, You're Okay*. A spate of other "self-help," feel-good books based on all kinds of theories and philosophies, most of them secular, followed.

Television and other forms of entertainment pushed the envelope even further than before. Shows that portrayed a cruder and more permissive lifestyle apart from traditional moral principles enjoyed great success and critical acclaim, including the groundbreaking *All in the Family*, a spin-off called *Maude*, *Three's Company*, and *Soap*. Rock and roll and the new sounds of disco music glorified one-night stands, while anti-God, profane George Carlin and the drug-obsessed duo Cheech and Chong reveled in the edgier side of humor. Public censors tried to keep the lid on this Pandora's box, but the outcry against them led to looser standards on the public airwaves.

A philosophy known as "postmodernism" began to take hold in mainstream American culture in the early 1970s, and it quickly began to replace time-honored Christian values. While modernists, including pragmatists, had sought the truth in a rational way, postmodernists said that truth wasn't something humans could attain, that it was relative. Everything flowed out of the individual's perspective, not from a universal source of truth, and each person's opinion was just as valid as someone else's. In the pluralistic society that America had become, the postmodernists thought that evangelism was the epitome of arrogance because it promoted the idea that Christianity was more right than other religions.

Before this era, Americans used to believe that a person could subscribe to universal truth and still allow other people to have their own point of view. Beginning in the 1970s, tolerance became mandatory for everyone except those who said there was, in fact, an objectively right view. In other words, there was no right view except the view that there was no right view! In addition, postmodernists were very big on emotion, since life couldn't be based on reason. They also disdained the idea of human progress, pointing to the sorry history of the twentieth century.

Two of the main proponents of this system were the French philosophers Jacques Derrida and Michel Foucault. Their viewpoints, aided by a ubiquitous media, eventually filtered down to even the smallest towns in America. Derrida believed that truth was simply one person's interpretation against another while Foucault said that all interpretation was fixed by those in power and was an exercise of power. In such a climate, it became very difficult to talk in terms of right and wrong. The concept of biblical authority took a beating as Americans began to see the Bible as one more book in one more religious tradition among many others. Since truth could not be arrived at, life's real significance, said postmodernists, was in relationships. Paradoxically, American families experienced unprecedented fragmentation during the '70s and afterward. Charles Colson, who became a Christian and an apologist for the faith in the early part of the decade, said, "When enough people hold to [moral relativity], this line of reasoning produces dramatic results in a nation's public values."[2] And it did.

✌◦◦✌

The ways in which Americans thought about heaven and hell began to change profoundly, including a new way of categorizing what happens after death. For example, heaven retained its popularity in this anything-goes era, but beliefs about who was going there and why became progressively more universalistic. Part of this shift came because of a changing perception of the nature of God. Most Americans rejected the idea of a vengeful deity, whom they referred to as the "God of the Old Testament" with its wars, plagues, and sacrifices, and embraced instead the "New Testament God" of love and grace. Even the most traditional Christians began to think this way, ignoring that Jesus Himself, whom they saw as the personification of love, spoke more about judgment and hell than anyone else in the Bible. Nevertheless, the very idea of a coming judgment no longer captured the beliefs, or the attention, of the majority of Americans.

Two prevalent ideas about life after death—one could no longer simply speak in terms of the doctrines of heaven and hell—were advanced by a blockbuster movie, a series of books, and the media's reporting of "near-death experiences." The film *Star Wars* appeared in 1977 with its catchphrase, "May the Force be with you." The Force was an impersonal power source, a substitute for the God of the Bible, and when someone died, he became one with it. He also gained the ability to communicate with those who were still alive. According to Obi-Wan Kenobi, a main character in the film, "The Force is what gives a Jedi his power. It's an energy field created by all living things. It surrounds us, and penetrates us. It binds the galaxy together."[3] The Force also had a dark side; the Jedi Knight Darth Vader had connected with it and gone bad. Although fictional, the idea of a Force appealed to many Americans who found themselves in need of a new concept of God to fit their postmodern lives.

In 1975, psychiatrist Raymond Moody added to the new wave of God-thought when he published *Life After Life* in which he chronicled the experiences of over one hundred people who were pronounced clinically dead, then went on to survive. He said each of them underwent similar occurrences, which he coined "near-death experiences." A sudden increase of similar titles took place in the following years, including Melvin Morse's *Closer to the Light*. The common denominator in those books was how each person encountered a light, often at the end of a tunnel. Many also reported meetings with a Christlike or angelic being who said that sin was not a problem, there was no hell, all people were welcome in heaven, and all religions provided equally valid ways to God.

Rather than drawing people closer to God, however, those working with, or having had, near-death experiences most often became universalistic or stopped believing in an afterlife. Raymond Moody himself said he didn't know if there really was life after death. At one point in his career, he developed something called a "psychomanteum," which was a re-created oracle in the ancient Greek tradition that people used to encounter dead spirits. He thought that by doing so he could try to re-create near-death experiences.

᭗᭜

The 1980s witnessed a continuing outgrowth of the philosophies of the '70s, but with greater intensity. American culture became more hardened to traditional values as, for example, increasing numbers of people openly lived together outside of marriage and appealed to abortionists when the outcome didn't go as planned. This decade also witnessed the rise of homosexual activism as "gays" sought greater civil rights and acceptance by mainstream society, the new scourge of the deadly AIDS virus notwithstanding. Not only were adults more sexually experimental and promiscuous, but their mores filtered down to the youngest Americans, who dressed and danced seductively in imitation of pop idols like Madonna and MTV videos. Both flaunted a flagrant, in-your-face sexuality; punk rock took this to lurid levels.

During that time, the church was no longer a fortress against the outside world; it was being transformed by the culture rather than setting the pace for it. Because God was increasingly viewed apart from any sense of accountability or judgment, many believers didn't worry about the penalty for their loosened moral standards. Two prominent Christians who compromised themselves, Jim Bakker and Jimmy Swaggert, got caught up in sexual and financial scandals that tore their lives and ministries apart. Parachurch organizations emerged to combat the growing permissiveness and vulgarity of American society. Among these was the Rev. Jerry Falwell's Moral Majority, a politically active group that helped deliver the evangelical vote for Ronald Reagan in the 1980 presidential election. Also gaining in strength were Pat Robertson's Christian Broadcast Network, including CBN University (renamed Regent University in 1989), the Christian Coalition, and James Dobson's Focus on the Family.

The mainline Protestant churches fared especially poorly during this period. From 1965 to 1990, they lost between one-fifth and one-third of their members. One study concluded, "Never before had any large religious body in this country lost members steadily for so many years."[4] The more liberal fellowships were not providing "clear-cut, compelling answers to questions concerning the meaning of life." Nor were they holding their members accountable for their behavior, according to the laws of the church bodies. The report concluded,

> In short, strong religions foster a level of commitment that binds
> members to the group; weak religions have low levels of commitment
> and are unable to resist influences that lower it even further. Somehow,
> in the course of the past century, these churches lost the will or the
> ability to teach the Christian faith and what it requires to a succession of
> younger cohorts in such a way as to command their allegiance.[5]

Although evangelical Christian churches and various forms of media oriented to that audience grew strongly, in the secular media Christians were under constant attack and often ridiculed. CNN, the first twenty-four-hour news network, emerged in the '80s. It was owned by Ted Turner, who openly held Christians in contempt, calling theirs a religion for losers. On the other networks a steady diet of anti-Christian stories stoked the fires of American resentment toward those who would dare tell them how to live. Whereas once society had regarded the church as a necessary component of maintaining high moral standards, now its leaders were increasingly viewing it as an obstacle to people doing just whatever they wanted with whomever they wanted, whenever they wanted.

Hollywood tended to portray Christians in a negative way, as well as heaven in a more secular manner. In films like *Field of Dreams* and *Ghost*, people with unresolved issues got stuck between death and the hereafter. In *Field of Dreams* a voice, whose source was never identified, instructed an Iowa farmer to build a ball field on his property so that the suspended, deceased members of the 1919 Chicago White Sox could play ball again. Never did the farmer wonder if the voice was God. There didn't seem to *be* a God in his world, except in the minds of some painfully narrow-minded townspeople who threatened to burn classical works of literature that they found objectionable, those whom his wife dubbed "Nazis." When one of the ballplayers asked if the mystical field was heaven, the farmer laughed and said, "Heaven is the place where dreams come true."

⚮

In spite of the unpopularity of Christianity in the mainstream culture of the '70s and '80s, most Americans considered themselves spiritual and sought new ways to satisfy their urge to connect with God apart from traditional churches or synagogues. New Age religion fulfilled that desire in many ways. Beginning in the '70s in fringe groups promoting astrology, UFO sightings, crystals, and auras, by the '80s New Age spirituality had become much more sophisticated. Certainly, actress Shirley MacLaine's 1983 *Out on a Limb* that chronicled her journey to belief that she was, in fact, God, and Anthony Robbins's *Awaken the Giant Within* gave legitimacy to the movement. Other celebrities like George Harrison, John Travolta, Michael Jackson, and David Carradine also gave it credibility. This brand of spirituality is syncretistic, a spiritual smorgasbord from which an individual could select whatever of its aspects were most beneficial to him. Among those were astrology and the occult, the use of crystals as power sources for healing and energy, channeling spirit guides, belief in reincarnation and karma, secret knowledge, Eastern mysticism, and pantheism. New Age adherents came to believe that since God created everything, everything was part of God. According to Christians Bob and Gretchen Passantino, "It's only a short step to the Hindu holy man who takes cow dung and smears 'God' in his hair."[6]

New Age adherents fit beautifully into American society as they sought a religion that would nurture their spirits without making moral demands. As in *Star Wars* with its nebulous "Force," this religion was big on relationships and emotion while disdaining any kind of final judgment. Everyone would get to a perfect place known as heaven—not necessarily the Christian concept of it—because everyone was basically good—and everyone was basically God, after all. Therefore, there was no need for any kind of punishment or hell. Jesuit John L. Thomas once said, "To deny the existence of Hell is implicitly to deny the need for redemption."[7] Jesus, then, was one of several holy men who came to reveal

God to humanity, a great prophet and teacher, but not the Savior Christians made Him out to be.

In the early part of the twentieth century, modernists swept clean the miraculous element in Christian belief, casting doubts on God's supernatural activity. By the 1970s and '80s, however, many Americans were instead filling their lives with mediums, horoscopes, crystals, and channeling in order to discover more about and direct their futures. People have an innate need to connect with the wonder-working, supernatural, awesome God, and if they do not, they will fill that desire with paltry substitutes.

∽o∾

It's interesting to see how the media covered, and people responded to, the deaths of various people during this jumbled period. It was a time when some Christians still had a strong, orthodox faith, others had doubts, and many more Americans began to believe in completely different teachings about the afterlife. On the one hand, there was the tragic death of baseball star Roberto Clemente at the end of December 1972. The Latino legend went on a relief mission to deliver supplies after an earthquake struck Nicaraugua. The overburdened DC-7 crashed shortly after taking off, and the thirty-eight-year-old's body was never recovered. A series of ecumenical services and Masses followed. An article in *The New Pittsburgh Courier* said, "We bow our head in prayer for the soul of Roberto Clemente. We offer our sincere condolence to his wife and family. . . . We say Roberto Clemente was a truly great man. May his soul rest in peace."[8]

Two other plane crashes claimed the lives of American celebrities in the '70s, including popular singer/songwriter Jim Croce, who sang "Operator" and "Time in a Bottle" to the top of the music charts. After his death on September 20, 1973, one reporter made a reference to Croce's musical spirit living on. Although Croce was raised Roman Catholic, he had converted to Judaism when he got married to his Jewish wife. On

August 2, 1979, New York Yankees All-Star catcher Thurman Munson died while piloting his private plane. Team owner George Steinbrenner created a plaque in Munson's honor for the Yankees' Monument Park. It read: "Our captain and leader has not left us, today, tomorrow, this year, next. Our endeavors will reflect our love and admiration for him."

Finally, the man who asked people to imagine life without heaven, hell, or religion, John Lennon, was shot to death on the night of December 8, 1980, outside his New York apartment building. Mourners quickly gathered around the world to pay their respects. Lennon's widow, Yoko Ono, announced that there would be no funeral, but instead a brief vigil on the 14th in which people could observe ten minutes of silence and pray for him, and for the world. It was estimated that millions did so globally, including around one hundred thousand who congregated in Central Park where the "service" ended with the playing of "Imagine" over loudspeakers. It wasn't clear to what God they had been praying, but one small sign held by a fan confidently proclaimed, "John Lennon lives."

In each case, there were references to those men living on in some vague way, but without any basis for how or why. Still on the horizon was the now-familiar phrase about them being "up there looking down on us." That began to change somewhere around the end of the '80s and the beginning of the '90s after universalism, syncretism, and a sentimental emphasis on emotions had put deep roots into the soil of American beliefs about heaven and hell. One turning point was the death of the *Challenger* astronauts in January 1986.

Late on the morning of January 28, the space shuttle blasted off from its launch pad at Cape Kennedy. Just a little over one minute into its ascent, the *Challenger* exploded, to the horror of those who had enthusiastically cheered its journey, including the parents of the first teacher in space, Christa McAuliffe. Seven astronauts perished that day, and the nation went into "a concert of grief," to borrow Sydney Ahlstrom's phrase, that lasted for days as the disaster replayed constantly over the airwaves. President Reagan was preparing for that night's State of the

Union address when he heard the news, but instead he spoke to the nation that afternoon about the disaster. In his moving speech, he quoted a sonnet by an American serviceman who had died in World War II. The president said, "We will never forget them, nor the last time we saw them, this morning, as they prepared for their journey and waved goodbye and 'slipped the surly bonds of earth' to 'touch the face of God.'"[9]

Memorial services were held in communities around the country, and Americans flew their flags at half-staff in honor of the astronauts. In the towns and cities in which the seven had been raised, there were also services in their honor. At one for Christa McAuliffe, her fellow teacher Charles Sposato remarked, "Christa McAuliffe is infinite because she is in our hearts." Ohio Governor Richard Celeste told Judith Resnik's parents at a service at Akron's Temple Israel, "She knew she would be at home in space. And she was. And she is." The Rev. Jesse Jackson told mourners of Ron McNair, he "belongs to the ages now." At the main memorial service for all seven in Houston, President Reagan referred to "God's promise of eternal life" as if the astronauts had all believed in Christ:

> Dick, Mike, Judy, El, Ron, Greg and Christa—your families and your country mourn your passing. We bid you goodbye. We will never forget you. For those who knew you well and loved you, the pain will be deep and enduring. A nation, too, will long feel the loss of her seven sons and daughters, her seven good friends. We can find consolation only in faith, for we know in our hearts that you who flew so high and so proud now make your home beyond the stars, safe in God's promise of eternal life.[10]

There was a subtle implication in the understandably poignant tributes to the astronauts that those good, brave, and dedicated public servants couldn't have gone anywhere else but to a good and loving God in heaven. It was obvious that the majority of Americans still felt their need of God and the promise of a better life to come at such a time.

17

FROM HERE TO
ETERNITY

It makes sense that people die in their sixties of cancer, sad but understandable. When Jackie Kennedy passed away on May 19, 1994, Americans were especially sad because they had come to love and admire her. Senator Edward Kennedy's office issued a statement saying, "Jackie was part of our family and part of our hearts for 40 wonderful and unforgettable years, and she will never really leave us."[1] Many other memories and tributes followed for the former First Lady, including journalist Lance Morrow's assessment of her very public life and how it related to her death:

> And for all the fragility she may have suggested in the big, round
> sunglasses and the head scarf, she wore some inner armoring; she
> possessed an eerie talent . . . to make herself disappear, to dematerialize.
> If you saw her on the street, she would seem to abstract herself out of
> public attention, a kind of elegant vanishing. She would be, as she finally
> is now . . . elsewhere.[2]

Although he didn't speculate on just where she went, the funeral at her Manhattan church emphasized the Roman Catholic understanding of gaining heaven through Jesus Christ. While it was sad that she died at a relatively young age by today's standards, it was not tragic. There was the usual extensive news coverage of her life and death, but it was nothing compared to the outpouring of grief that followed the tragic events of a mid-summer evening five years later.

On July 16, 1999, thirty-eight-year-old John F. Kennedy Jr., his wife of three years, and her sister set out in a Piper Saratoga from New Jersery to attend the wedding of his cousin Rory on Cape Cod. They never arrived. Kennedy lost control of the aircraft, which plummeted into the ocean. Initially news reports conveyed hope that they might be rescued. It seemed too terrible to believe that yet another heartrending death would hound the Kennedy family. But when their bodies were recovered from the sea, a national torrent of emotion followed, very much like what happened when Princess Diana died two years earlier.

The media hailed JFK Jr. as "America's Prince" and the heir to "Camelot." The iconic image of him at age three saluting his father's casket appeared all over newspapers, magazines, and during many hours of television coverage. Thousands of floral tributes, balloons, cards, and other mementos appeared at a makeshift memorial at Kennedy's Tribeca apartment. As people lamented over "what might have been"—the next President Kennedy perhaps—there was no question in most minds that he and the other two had gone to heaven. In his eulogy at a shipboard burial service, Senator Kennedy said, "We thank the millions who have rained blossoms down on John's memory. He and his bride have gone to be with his mother and father, where there will never be an end to love."[3] This supposition was likely based on both the Catholic Church's belief that baptized members go to heaven, as well as on the prevailing cultural notion that "good" people go there.

A popular television show at the time of JFK Jr.'s death played into American society's universalistic inclinations. In *Touched by an Angel*, three heavenly messengers assisted people during especially trying or critical times. Andrew was the "angel of death," whose job it was to escort the dying to heaven. There was a tacit assumption that any decent person would go there because God is loving toward everyone He has created.

During the period of mourning for John Kennedy Jr., Kevin Merida observed,

> There is a ritual that accompanies public death, a distinctly American science of public grieving and public reflection and public analysis. Public death has come to be defined as the tragic loss of those so famous or important or singular that their sudden departure triggers the ritual.
>
> John F. Kennedy and Martin Luther King Jr . . . Elvis and John Lennon . . . the astronauts of the space shuttle Challenger and the kids of Columbine High . . . Princess Di and now JFK Jr., whose body was retrieved yesterday from underwater plane wreckage and brought back to land.[4]

That level of grief isn't limited to the rich and influential. There have been high levels of public bereavement following the 1993 attack on the World Trade Center; the 1995 bombing of the federal building in Oklahoma City; the September 11, 2001, attacks; the 2004 tsunami; Hurricane Katrina; and the shootings at Virginia Tech. Back in the 1950s, Anne Morrow Lindbergh observed in her *Gift from the Sea* that in an earlier era, people weren't as burdened by what happened in places removed from their own experience because they didn't know about them. In the '50s, however, which seem so quiescent compared to today's continual bombardment of information, Americans were joined much more to a global community and thus connected to tragedies that were unrelated to them. How much more is this the case now with our high-speed communication, when people barely catch up with one event or trend before the next one begins? Americans are participant bystanders who end up grieving over people they've never met but with whom they feel an association. Regarding the JFK Jr. death, Kevin Merida concluded, "Public death has become one of the binding American experiences, giving strangers something to talk about in a culture in which individuals are increasingly distanced."[5]

∽o∾

People often say about those who died, "He's gone to a better place," "She is always with me," or "He is up there looking down on us." Overwhelmingly, Americans believe that with few exceptions, everyone goes to heaven. A small number say there is no such place. Countless people from various cultural backgrounds and religious traditions are in agreement about this. There are several reasons. With mass communication that reaches into virtually every home, Americans have conformed to a common language and a common viewpoint. In addition, trends stretching back over the past several decades have eroded biblical orthodoxy about the afterlife. Public education at all levels also trains Americans not to judge other people. Since there is no concept of sin, there can be no wrong to be punished. The culture plays into the natural state of rebellion that exists toward God's precepts, especially that Jesus is the only way to be united with Him here and in the life to come.

Postmodern Americans place a high value on emotion and sentiment. Therefore, they take what society gives them, mix it with the memory of their own faith traditions, then syncretize it with whatever teaching offers the most satisfaction or the best feelings. Columnist Ellen Goodman cited a study by the Pew Forum on Religion and Public Life in which thirty-five thousand Americans shared their religious experiences. The conclusion showed that 44 percent of Americans do not belong to the same religious institution in which they were raised. Says Goodman, "The researchers describe a 'vibrant marketplace where individuals pick and choose religions that meet their needs.' They surf their options."[6]

∽o∽

A prevailing American observation about dead loved ones and celebrities is, first of all, that they are in heaven, then that they are "up there looking down" on us or are in some way present. In addition, some believe the dead are able to intervene on behalf of others or to let us know that they aren't gone forever—a fundamental human need that transcends time and cultures. In a 2003 "Family Circus" comic strip, a birthday party for the father was shown. As his wife put the last of the candles on the cake he said, "When I was little, every year on October 5th my father would play his guitar while everybody sang happy birthday to me." As his children and spouse sang to him, up in heaven his father sat on a cloud strumming his guitar. One of the children exclaimed, "While we were singin' I heard a lot of strummin' and plunkin'!" His sister shouted, "Me too!" while their dad looked heavenward with a wistful smile.[7]

While this provides reassurance to those who have lost someone special, is there any reliable basis for believing it, and how did Americans arrive at that idea in the first place? Pat Robertson, founder and chairman of the Christian Broadcasting Network, thinks it represents a Hollywood version of the afterlife. "I can't put my finger on it, but there have been several movie plots, usually humorous in nature, that have people who are deceased and are hanging around and looking down, and we've adopted a Hollywood view of it."[8] Although the entertainment industry and Christianity are often at odds, there actually is something in the church's tradition that has also played a part in this image of heaven.

"The Apostles' Creed," whose origins stretch back to the early centuries of Christianity, affirms that there is a "communion of saints." A "saint" is simply one who has been saved by Jesus Christ and sanctified or made holy by His death on the cross; consequently, there are living saints and dead saints. The Roman Catholic Church encourages its people to pray to dead saints to intervene in their lives and/or seek God's particular favor about some situation. It maintains that all believers are linked together in Christ whether they are dead or alive and that those who are dead have a closer relationship with God. Protestants maintain, however, that while there is a spiritual link in Christ between all the faithful, dead and living, it doesn't extend to their actually communicating with each other. They also believe that people should pray to God alone.

Others point to certain Bible passages to support the idea that the dead in Christ are somehow aware of the living, and possibly able to assist them. Randy Alcorn says, "The Bible makes evident heaven's inhabitants see, to some extent, what's happening on earth."[9] He cites Hebrews 12:1: "Therefore, since we are surrounded by such a great cloud of witnesses, let us throw off everything that hinders and the sin that so easily entangles, and let us run with perseverance the race marked out for us." Alcorn says this alludes to Greek athletic contests in which fans watched their heroes while seated high up in stadiums. For the Christian, "The 'great cloud of witnesses' refers to saints whose previous accomplishments on life's playing field are now part of our rich history. The imagery suggests those saints, the spiritual 'athletes' of old, now watch and cheer us on from the great stadium of heaven that looks down on the field of earth."[10]

The deceased witnesses in Hebrews 12:2, however, are not witnessing what is happening to their loved ones. Instead, what they are actually witnessing to is the Lord Jesus Christ.[11] According to Christopher Sutton:

> When you consider Hebrews 11, you see that there were many people in the past who were faithful. Although they are now dead, their lives are an encouragement to us to be faithful, too. Their lives can be stacked up all around us as evidence to persevere in the faith. There is no indication here that the deceased can see us, observe our activities, or fellowship with us. . . . It occurs to me that if people in heaven could see us down here on earth that it would not be heaven for them. To look down and see the vices of mankind would cause a pure heart to weep and experience sorrow. Revelation 21:4 tells us that in heaven there will be ". . . no more death or mourning or crying or pain . . . ." In short, I do not believe that the saints in heaven are watching us. They are surely preoccupied with Jesus and their glorious home![12]

The prevailing idea in our culture that people in heaven can see and influence what is happening on earth provides reassurance, however false, that they are still somehow linked with their loved ones who are still alive. However, the Bible emphasizes that those who go to heaven are now part of a new order of things, and that the old order has passed away (Revelation 21:4). For example, Jesus said that there would be no marriage in heaven; that is part of the old order (Mark 12:25). With all tears and pain and loss behind them, heaven's citizens no longer have consciousness of what is happening on earth. Rather, their focus is on the Lord Jesus. Believers in Him go to heaven to serve Him and to see His face, and they will reign with Him forever (Revelation 22:3–5). The beloved in Christ go to heaven so that they might live with Him and be united with Him (1 Thessalonians 5:10; Romans 6:5; 2 Timothy 2:11; 1 Corinthians 15:52; Philippians 1:23). When Martha grieved over the death of her brother, Lazarus, she shared her hope with Jesus that Lazarus would live again in the resurrection, *not* that she would be with him again some day. Then Jesus told her that He was the resurrection, that He was the life. Those who are in Him will never die. That is the believer's blessed hope. When loved ones share that hope, they *are* forever linked, in Christ.

American society is oriented toward emotion and relativism, both of which lead people outside the Christian faith, as well as increasing numbers within it, to believe that all good and sincere people go to heaven. Most people believe they are good because they do whatever is right in their own eyes. Since no one is supposed to have the authority to say what is right and wrong, people are left to define those categories for themselves. Pat Robertson says, "I think we have developed a culture of feeling good, and nobody ever gets told that they're not living up to a standard. It's in the economy, the workplace, schools. In our society there just doesn't seem to be consequences for people's actions. We talk a lot about rewards, but not punishments."[13]

One of the main authorities of American life whose opinion many follow to the letter is talk show host and entrepreneur Oprah Winfrey. In an interview with a rap star she spoke with great conviction when she said we all know "there are many paths to God."[14] An orthodox Christian might find it effortless to dismiss this comment, but is that same person aware of how far universalism has spread within the church itself? One of the most popular praise songs in America is "Come, Now Is the Time to Worship," which contains a strong implication that all will be saved in the end. The lyrics contain a reference to Philippians 2:9–11: "Therefore God exalted him to the highest place and gave him the name that is above every name, that at the name of Jesus every knee should bow, in heaven and on earth and under the earth, and every tongue confess that Jesus Christ is Lord, to the glory of God the Father." The implication in this song is that everyone is going to be saved when Christ reveals Himself in His glory at the end of time, but "the greatest treasure remains for those who gladly choose him now."[15] If the word "only" was substituted for "greatest," that would be a more accurate portrayal of Philippians 2. This Scripture actually means, "The man who had become obedient to death was now the world's sovereign. In his name, i.e., acknowledging his authority, all will submit to him because they cannot do otherwise."[16]

∾o∾

A 2004 Gallup poll revealed that 81 percent of Americans believe in heaven, a statistic that has remained steady for fifty years. Seventy percent said they thought there was a hell, but few people thought they would be going there. Even so, Jeffrey Burton Brown has found that "what people mean by [heaven] has changed an awful lot." For example, some who believe in heaven don't actually believe in God.[17] Likewise, *AARP* magazine commissioned its own survey of Americans over the age of fifty about life after death. Among its conclusions, "Most Americans believe they will be saved no matter what they are."[18] According to that survey, 77 percent believe in life after death with 86 percent of older Americans saying there's a heaven and 70 percent, there is a hell. Eighty-eight percent of respondents believe they'll go to heaven, 40 percent said people who are bad or who have sinned go to hell, and 17 percent said that people who don't believe in Jesus go there. Interestingly, of those age fifty and older, 23 percent believe in reincarnation, enough of the population to make a song like Terri Clark's "In My Next Life" acceptable.[19] The article concluded, "Generally, the traditionally clear Christian vision of Heaven has declined, while the vaguer visions of the continuation of life have taken its place."[20] A case in point is the belief of author Edwin Shrake who, during a medical emergency, said he had an "after-life experience" that taught him "there is no heaven and hell, no Christian, Jewish, Muslim or Buddhist. Life is the gasoline that runs our engine. The machine breaks, but your spirit goes on."[21]

This is what Americans are saying, but what are their pastors teaching from pulpits about heaven and hell? A Phoenix-based marketing research firm set out to answer that question by surveying seven hundred active ministers from several Protestant denominations. Ellison Research discovered that there were major differences between mainline and evangelical ministers. Of the evangelical pastors, 96 percent agreed strongly that Jesus was the only way, while just 65 percent of their mainline counterparts did so.[22] In addition, there are many variations within denominations regarding the characteristics of heaven and hell. Evangelicals generally teach that the believing dead are *with* Christ at death, although there is some debate among them about whether there is immediate consciousness or if that will occur at the second coming. Evangelicals believe that heaven is a glorious place where there is an absence of pain, disease, and distress, where people get new spiritual bodies and live eternally, in the presence of Jesus.

Conversely, hell is isolation from God, according to many pastors. The majority view throughout American history has been that hell is an eternal, horrific condition, and while that view is still prevalent, a growing number of evangelicals now think that those who reject Christ will be punished for an interval that is proportional to their sins, then they will be completely annihilated, no longer to exist in any form. Theology professor Clark Pinnock is a chief spokesman for the latter view. He also believes that people might still be able to accept Christ "postmortem," saying, "Scripture does not require us to hold that the window of opportunity is slammed shut at death. The fate of some may be sealed at death; those, for example, who heard the gospel and declined the offer of salvation. But the fate of others is not sealed; babies, for example, who die in infancy."[23]

In mainline Protestant churches there are variations regarding what is currently taught, but they tend to be in considerable agreement with society's view of heaven and hell. The prevailing beliefs are that most people go to heaven—either a place or a state of being—while hell is mainly a concept, not a place of punishment, either temporary or eternal. Rather, the biblical writers who spoke of it were using metaphorical or mythological language to teach. Mainline Christians tend to believe that an individual should not be punished because they never heard the gospel or because they adhered to a different religious tradition, which would be irrational and unjust—certainly not the behavior of a loving God.

Roman Catholic and Eastern Orthodox churches regard heaven as a gift from God following whatever purification may be necessary in purgatory. Hell is reserved for all those who die alienated from God. According to the *The Handbook of Catholic Theology*, "To be in heaven means . . . to live in the company of God and Christ. . . . In the final analysis, we will not be *in* heaven but rather, as the one Christ, will ourselves *be* heaven."[24] In 1999, Pope John Paul II declared, "Hell is not a punishment imposed externally by God, but the condition resulting from attitudes and actions which people adopt in this life. . . . So eternal damnation is not God's work but is actually our own doing." He elaborated that while it is not a physical place, "hell is the state of those who freely and definitively separate themselves from God, the source of all life and joy."[25]

∽○∽

Most Americans have been loosened from the biblical moorings of their ancestors regarding afterlife beliefs and are picking and choosing from the leftovers whatever suits their emotional needs. They are content to believe that just about everyone goes to heaven without asking whether they are basing that conviction on anything reliable. They don't want to hear that they might be mistaken, and they aren't especially eager to delve into the subject of hell. God's eternal truth, however, presses upon us in spite of public opinion, and choices must be made. Jesus said, "Enter through the narrow gate. For wide is the gate and broad is the road that leads to destruction, and many enter through it. But small is the gate and narrow the road that leads to life, and only a few find it" (Matthew 7:13–14).

EPILOGUE

D oes what Americans believe about heaven and hell really matter? Does it make a significant difference in the way we live, and
die? During the earlier part of our history, in eras when disease often
swept lives away with barely enough time to prepare for the end, people
took comfort in the hope of heaven. They also looked forward to spend-
ing eternity in the presence of God along with their believing friends
and relatives. In addition, a healthy respect for a holy God, along with
a fear of hell, provided motivation for people to live according to biblical principles. Today most Americans, including many Christians, live
by their own rules without concern for present or future consequences.
Medical and technological advances have resulted in our living longer
and healthier than previous generations, and those we look up to, as well
as the mainstream media, tell us we have nothing to fear at death. Unless you're Adolf Hitler, Saddam Hussein, or some other truly despicable
person, you'll be going to a better place.

This ground is, however, sinking sand. The Christian hope of heaven
and the horror of hell are both real and appropriate, even for the twenty-
first century. This is what Americans have believed and acted upon
historically and what tenacious souls continue to accept as true. C. S.
Lewis wrote, "If you read history you will find that the Christians who did
the most for the present world were just those who thought most of the
next."[1] He gave as examples the apostles, who converted the degenerate

Roman Empire; British Christians, led by William Wilberforce, who
ended the slave trade; and American believers who helped stop slavery
and the mistreatment of the mentally ill, and who bettered the lot of prisoners, the handicapped, and the poor. They were the ones who first
promoted women's rights and civil rights for blacks, and today they are
fighting to bring an end to sex trafficking and the denigration of respect
for human life.

A further reason why a biblical belief in heaven and hell is valuable is
that it puts suffering in perspective. If we endure pain and heartbreak for
no apparent reason, if life really is without meaning or purpose, then we
should all be hand-wringing followers of Albert Camus who grit our teeth
and carry on to prove that we can. The Bible, however, is full of teachings
and examples that relate to God's purposes for the sorrows we bear in
this life, particularly how He uses them to conform us to the image of
Christ, to make us sensitive and helpful to others who are suffering, to
mature us, and to keep us looking toward the excellence of heaven.

Randy Alcorn believes that

> meditating on Heaven is a great pain reliever. It reminds us that
> suffering and death are temporary conditions. Our existence will not
> end in suffering and death—they are but a gateway to our eternal life of
> unending joy. The biblical doctrine of Heaven is about the future, but
> it has tremendous benefits here and now. If we grasp it, it will shift our
> center of gravity and radically change our perspective on life.[2]

Over forty years ago, Joni Eareckson Tada became a quadriplegic in a
diving accident. She was seventeen, and she wanted to end it all. By God's
grace and through the ministry of His people, Joni accepted her new reality and over the years has become a spokeswoman for the disabled. In
her book *When God Weeps*, she speaks about one of the purposes for af-
flictions: By tasting hell in this life we are driven to ponder what may face
us in the next. In this way, our trials may be our greatest mercies. For
some of us, they become God's roadblocks on our headlong rush to hell.[3]

The Bible makes it clear that the suffering that believers in Christ endure in this life is nothing compared to the bliss of heaven. Second Corinthians 4:17–18 says, "For our light and momentary troubles are achieving for us an eternal glory that far outweighs them all. So we fix our eyes not on what is seen, but on what is unseen. For what is seen is temporary, but what is unseen is eternal." Promises like this gave Cynthia and Joe Drenth hope and meaning in the midst of deep trials. Joe is legally blind, and during his first year of marriage, his bride was diagnosed with an aggressive form of ovarian cancer. He says:

> We knew that our time together on earth would be short and our dream
> of growing a strong family for the Lord would not be realized. Our
> mission as a couple was transformed from the normal goal of bringing
> up the next generation of believers to being a model for those around us
> of how God's love and grace help us to endure suffering and death while
> praising the Lord and holding up the promise of eternal life through
> Jesus Christ.[4]

When they experienced inevitable slumps during Cynthia's battle with cancer, "an eternal perspective" strengthened them: "Whenever we reached low points of discouragement, prayer and love from our family and friends helped us regain our eternal perspective and see that her temporary ordeals were soon to be replaced by everlasting joy and happiness in the presence of Jesus."[5] Now that Cynthia has gone to her eternal home, the promise of heaven comforts Joe:

> The calming hand of God and the certainty in my heart that Cynthia is
> not dead but alive in Christ keeps me on task and allows me to deal with
> the most difficult memories. The pain of separation brought about by
> the death of a loved one is just as real for a Believer as for a non-Believer,
> but the Comforter sent by Jesus makes it bearable and the hope of
> seeing our loved one again dispels the despair that would otherwise be
> overwhelming. Our citizenship is in heaven, not on earth (Philippians
> 3:20), and may our lives and deaths be to the glory and honor of the Lord
> Most High.[6]

In an interview not long after the death of his beloved wife, Ruth, Billy Graham also spoke of the peace he found through his belief in the One who overcame hell and death. "Most of all," he said, "I take comfort in the Word of God, and in the hope we can have of eternal life in Heaven because of Christ's death and resurrection for us. I've preached this message almost all my life, and it means more to me now than ever before."[7]

While heaven gives believers a purpose in suffering, the existence of hell also serves a purpose: It ensures that justice will be served. Joni Eareckson Tada says, "Without hell, the 'why' behind so much pain will never be resolved. Without hell, there is ultimately no justice or fairness. For God to be God, for heaven to be heaven, there *must* be a hell. . . . Unless hell exists, there is no justice in the world."[8] She points to Hitler and his cohorts, those responsible for the monstrous anguish of millions and how "these people were never paid back remotely in proportion to the pain they caused."[9] Hell ensures that they will get what they deserve.

Pat Robertson says that in other eras of American history, "The whole concept of ultimate rewards and ultimate punishments had a great deal to do with conduct. [Today] people feel there are no consequences to their actions."[10] But there are. When this happens, when there is no truth outside of oneself, there is no moral deterrent, and, according to Charles Colson, "The overall decline undermines society's primary institutional supports. . . . Radical individualism and its resulting relativism destroy this self-restraint."[11] Robertson agrees that having a deterrent to immorality is important. "I think it matters a great deal, but again, people are taught that there are just no consequences to their actions, that nothing bad is ever going to happen to them. A discussion of hell is so unpopular." Nevertheless, people will respond to God's truth when the Holy Spirit convicts them. Robertson spoke of a *700 Club* program he hosted in which a man who said he'd gone to hell gave his testimony. Many people say they've seen glimpses of heaven, but this man spoke of the other place. During that time, he gave an invitation to accept Christ, and nearly twelve hundred called in. He said that it was one of the biggest responses the show had ever experienced.[12]

From time immemorial, all people everywhere have tried to find respite from their grief when a loved one dies, as well as hope for what comes next. Beverly Roberts Gaventa observes, "People in desperate pain will seek and grasp for comfort wherever they can find it, in an effort to manage the pain of loss."[13] Living with the hope of Jesus Christ to overcome sin and hell gives meaning and perspective to life, as well as hope, purpose in suffering, and a moral foundation for individuals and society. Believing that we get all this, and heaven too, apart from Christ, is the most dangerous kind of folly.

∽o∾

> And now, dear brothers and sisters, we want you to know what will happen to the believers who have died so you will not grieve like people who have no hope. For since we believe that Jesus died and was raised to life again, we also believe that when Jesus returns, God will bring back with him the believers who have died.
>
> We tell you this directly from the Lord: We who are still living when the Lord returns will not meet him ahead of those who have died. For the Lord himself will come down from heaven with a commanding shout, with the voice of the archangel, and with the trumpet call of God. First, the Christians who have died will rise from their graves. Then, together with them, we who are still alive and remain on the earth will be caught up in the clouds to meet the Lord in the air. Then we will be with the Lord forever. So encourage each other with these words.
>
> (1 Thessalonians 4:13–18 NLT)

NOTES

Chapter One: What Are We Thinking?

1. Evan Thomas, "The Day That Changed America," *Newsweek*, December 31–January 7, 2002, 42–71.
2. Ibid.
3. Ibid.
4. "This Day in History," http://www.history.com/this-day-in-history.do?action=Article&id=172.
5. ABC News, Nightline: In Remembrance, 1/4/03, http://abcnewsstore.go.com/webapp/wcs/stores/servlet/DSIProductDisplay?catalogId=11002&storeId=20051&productId=2006459&langId=-1&categoryId=100031.
6. "What Lives They Lived," *Newsweek*, December 31–January 7, 2003, 106–11.
7. *Philadelphia Inquirer,* July 30, 2003.
8. Madeline Drexler, "Under the Influence," *Good Housekeeping*, July 2003, 142–53.
9. Tim Russert, *Wisdom of Our Fathers* (New York: Random House, 2006), 220–21.

Chapter Two: Let's Start at the Very Beginning

1. Richard L. Greaves, Robert Zaller, Philip V. Cannistraro, and Rhoads Murphey, *Civilizations of the World: The Human Adventure* (New York: Harper & Row, 1990), 137.
2. Eugene Merrill, *Everlasting Dominion: A Theology of the Old Testament* (Nashville: Broadman & Holman, 2006), 209–16.
3. R. Laird Harris, Gleason Archer, and Bruce Waltke, *Theological Wordbook of the Old Testament,* vol. 2. (Chicago: The Moody Bible Institute, 1980), 893.
4. Ibid.
5. Ibid.
6. Greaves et al., 153.
7. John Boardman, Jasper Griffin, and Oswyn Murray, *The Oxford Dictionary of the Classical World* (Oxford: Oxford, 1986), 268.
8. Ibid., 267.
9. Ibid., 267–68.
10. Williston Walker, *A History of the Christian Church* (New York: Charles Scribner's Sons, 1970), 5–6.

11. Ibid., 6.

12. Boardman, Griffin, and Murray, 268.

13. M. L. Clarke, *The Roman Mind: Studies in the History of Thought From Cicero to Marcus Aurelius* (New York: W.W. Norton & Company, 1968), 62.

14. L. P. Wilkinson, *The Roman Experience* (New York: Alfred A. Knopf, Inc., 1974), 187.

15. Clarke, 85.

16. Ibid.

17. Walker, 10–11.

18. Wilkinson, 187.

19. Information taken from the following Web sites:
www.spanishome.com/mayas/religion
www.carmensandiego.com/products/time/aztecsc12/religion
www.meta-religion.com/world_Religions/Ancient_religions/South_america/Inca_religion.

20. Peter Farb, *Man's Rise to Civilization as Shown by the Indians of North America from Primeval Times to the Coming of the Industrial State* (New York: Dutton, 1968), 107.

21. James Merrell, *The Indians' New World: Catawbas and Their Neighbors from European Contact through the Era of Removal* (Chapel Hill, NC: The Institute of Early American History and Culture, Williamsburg, VA, 1989), 264–65.

22. Ibid.

23. Ibid.

Chapter Three: American Origins

1. Peter Marshall and David Manuel, *The Light and the Glory* (Grand Rapids, MI: Fleming H. Revell, 1977), 252.

2. Ibid., 253.

3. Ibid.

4. Peter A. Lillback, *George Washington's Sacred Fire* (Bryn Mawr, PA: Providence Forum Press, 2006), 831.

5. Peter A. Lillback, interview with the author, November 12, 2007.

6. This section on Pocahontas and John Rolfe is adapted from Rebecca Price Janney, *Great Stories in American History* (Camp Hill, PA: Horizon Books, 1998), 9–11.

7. Ann Coulter, *Treason* (New York: Crown Forum, 2003), 288.

8. Kenneth Scott Latourette, *A History of Christianity: Reformation to Present, Volume 2: AD 1500–1975* (Peabody, MA: Prince Press, 2000), 703.

9. Ibid.

10. Ibid., 705.

11. Ibid., 752.

12. Ibid., 756.

13. Samuel Eliot Morison, Henry Steele Commager, and William E. Leuchtenburg, *The Growth of the American Republic* (New York: Oxford University Press, 1969), 50–51.

14. John A. Garraty and Robert A. McCaughey, *The American Nation* (New York: Harper & Row, 1987), 22.

Chapter Four: Fanning the Flames

1. Nancy Isenberg and Andrew Burstein, *Mortal Remains: Death in Early America* (Philadelphia: University of Pennsylvania Press, 2003), 1.

2. Description of Philip C. Almond's *Heaven and Hell in Enlightenment England* (Cambridge: Cambridge University Press, 1994), http://www.cup.cam.ac.uk/us/catalogue/catalogue.asp?isbn=0521453712.

3. Isenberg and Burstein, 31.

4. Ibid., 60–61.

5. Peter Marshall and David Manuel, *The Light and the Glory* (Grand Rapids, MI: Fleming H. Revell, 1977), 240.

6. Ibid., 249.

7. Jonathan Edwards, *A Faithful Narrative of the Surprising Work of God* (Grand Rapids, MI: Baker Book House, 1979), 23.

8. Ibid., 15.

9. Martin E. Marty, *Righteous Empire: The Protestant Experience in America* (New York: Harper & Row, 1970), 80.

10. Edwards, 16–17.

11. Ibid., 28.

12. Jonathan Edwards, "Sinners in the Hands of an Angry God," preached in Enfield, Connecticut, on July 8, 1741, Christian Classics Ethereal Library, http://www.ccel.org/ccel/edwards/sermons.sinners.html.

13. F. L. Chapell, *The Great Awakening of 1740* (city: American Baptist Publication Society, 1903).

14. Colleen McDannell and Bernhard Lang, *Heaven: A History* (Hartford: Yale Nota Bene, 2001), 177–78.

15. Marshall and Manuel, 247.

16. Ibid.

17. Rev. Gilbert Tennent, "The Danger of an Unconverted Ministry," http://www.sound-doctrine.net/Classic_Sermons/Gilbert%20Tennent/danger_of_unconverted.htm.

18. Rebecca Price Janney, "George Whitefield: From School Dropout to Open-Air Evangelist," Glimpses for Kids, http://chi.gospelcom.net/kids/glimpsesforkids/gfk024.php.

19. Samuel Eliot Morison, Henry Steele Commager, and William E. Leuchtenburg, *The Growth of the American Republic* (New York: Oxford University Press, 1969), 107–8.

20. Carl Van Doren, *Benjamin Franklin* (New York: Viking Press, 1938), 131.

21. Ibid., 136.

22. Ibid., 138.

23. M. Lincoln Schuster, *A Treasury of the World's Greatest Letters* (New York: Simon and Schuster, 1940), 163–64.

24. Marshall and Manuel, 250.

25. Ibid., 252.

26. Ibid., 253.

27. George Whitefield, "The Folly and Danger of Parting with Christ for the Pleasures and Profits of Life," Christian Classics Ethereal Library, http://www.ccel.org/ccel/whitefield/sermons.xxiv.html.

Chapter Five: You Say You Want a Revolution

1. *The New England Primer*, 1777 edition, http://www.sacred-texts.com/chr/nep/1777/index.htm.
2. Dr. Peter A. Lillback, interview with the author, November 12, 2007.
3. See also Peter Lillback's excellent study of George Washington, *George Washington's Sacred Fire* (Bryn Mawr, PA: Providence Forum Press, 2006).
4. Martin E. Marty, *Righteous Empire: The Protestant Experience in America* (New York: Harper & Row, 1970), 1.
5. Peter Marshall and David Manuel, *The Light and the Glory* (Grand Rapids, MI: Fleming H. Revell, 1977), 310.
6. Rebecca Price Janney, *Great Women in American History* (Camp Hill, PA: Horizon Books, 1996), 8.
7. Ibid.
8. Ibid., 11.
9. Ibid., 12.
10. Jeff Jacoby, "Our Lives, Our Fortunes, and Our Sacred Honor," *Jewish World Review*, July 3, 2000.
11. Marshall and Manuel, 321.
12. Ibid., 322.
13. Ibid.
14. Ibid., 323.
15. Ibid.
16. Ibid., 326.
17. Rebecca Price Janney, *Great Letters in American History* (Camp Hill, PA: Horizon Books, 2000), 52.
18. "Religion and the Founding of the American Republic," Library of Congress exhibition, http://www.loc.gov/exhibits/religion/rel03.html.
19. Lillback interview.
20. Peter A. Lillback, *George Washington's Sacred Fire* (Bryn Mawr, PA: Providence Forum Press, 2006), 38.

Chapter Six: Alternate Lifestyles

1. John A. Garraty and Robert A. McCaughey, *The American Nation: A History of the United States*, 6th ed. (New York: Harper & Row, 1987), 349–51.
2. Sydney E. Ahlstrom, *A Religious History of the American People*, vol. 1 (Garden City, NY: Image Books, 1975), 593–94.
3. Ibid.
4. Ibid., 594.
5. Ibid., 596.
6. Ibid., 597.
7. Robley Edward Whitson, ed., *The Shakers: Two Centuries of Spiritual Reflection* (New York: Paulist Press, 1983), 136.
8. Charles Nordhoff, *The Communistic Societies of the United States* (1875), http://www.sacred-texts.com/utopia/csus/csus14.htm.

9. *The Shaker Manifesto* XII, 3, 1882, 49–50.

10. Anna White and Leila Sarah Taylor, *Shakerism* (Columbus, OH: Press of F. J. Heer, 1905), 102.

11. George Wallingford Noyes, *Religious Experience of John Humphrey Noyes, Founder of the Oneida Community* (New York: Macmillan, 1923), 49.

12. Ibid., 295.

13. Ibid., 416.

14. "Robert Owen," Wikipedia, http://en.wikipedia.org/wiki/Robert_Owen.

15. The Afterlife: Beliefs of Individual Christian Denominations, "Mormons," http://www.religioustolerance.org/heav_hel3.htm#lds.

16. Ibid.

17. Ibid., quoting *The Doctrine and Covenants of the Church of Jesus Christ of Latter-Day Saints*, 76:102.

18. Ibid., quoting *Doctrine and Covenants*, 76:70–107.

19. Ibid.

20. Ibid., quoting *Doctrine and Covenants,* 76:84.

21. Ibid.

22. Douglas James Davies, *An Introduction to Mormonism* (New York: Cambridge, 2003), 174.

Chapter Seven: That Old-Time Religion

1. *Posthumous Works of the Reverend and Pious James M'Gready, Minister of the Gospel, in Henderson, Kentucky,* ed. Rev. James Smith, 2 vols. (Louisville, KY: W.W. Worsley, 1831), http://www.cumberland.org/hfcpc/McGreaBK.htm.

2. Sydney E. Ahlstrom, *A Religious History of the American People*, vol. 1 (Garden City, NY: Image Books, 1975), 525.

3. Ibid., 526.

4. Peter Marshall and David Manuel, *The Light and the Glory* (Grand Rapids, MI: Fleming H. Revell, 1977), 67.

5. Ibid., 68.

6. Ibid., 69.

7. Bernard A. Weisberger, *They Gathered at the River* (Boston: Little, Brown & Co., 1958), 96–97; quoted in Marshall and Manuel, 305–30.

8. Marshall and Manuel, 306.

9. Charles Grandison Finney, *An Autobiography* (Westwood, NJ: Fleming H. Revell, Co., 1908), 9.

10. Marshall and Manuel, 307.

11. Charles Grandison Finney, "Stewardship, Sermon IX, Luke xvi.2," in *Sermons on Important Subjects*, http://www.gospeltruth.net/1836SOIS/09sois_stewardship.htm.

12. Charles Grandison Finney, "The Rich Man and Lazarus," *The Oberlin Evangelist*, November 9, 1853, http://www.gospeltruth.net/1853OE/531109_richman_lazarus.htm.

13. Marshall and Manuel, 102.

14. Charles E. Cuningham, *Timothy Dwight, 1752–1817* (New York: Macmillan, 1942), no page number.

15. Ibid., 287.

16. Ibid., 325.
17. Charles Grandison Finney, "Stewardship, Sermon IX, Luke xvi.2," in *Sermons on Important Subjects*, http://www.gospeltruth.net/1836SOIS/09sois_stewardship.htm.
18. Rebecca Price Janney, *Great Stories in American History* (Camp Hill, PA: Christian Publications, 1998), 105.
19. Ibid.
20. Lyman Beecher, "The Nature and Occasions of Intemperance," in *Six Sermons on Intemperance* (Boston: T. R. Marvin, 1828), http://www.iath.virginia.edu/utc/sentimnt/sneslbat.html.
21. Marshall and Manuel, 394–95.

Chapter Eight: Knocking on Heaven's Door
1. Nancy Isenberg and Andrew Burstein, eds., *Mortal Remains: Death in Early America* (Philadelphia: University of Pennsylvania Press, 2003), 177.
2. Ibid.
3. Ibid.
4. Irwin Unger, *These United States: The Questions of Our Past*, 6th ed. (Englewood Cliffs, NJ: Prentice Hall, 1995), 642.
5. Isenberg and Burstein, 177.
6. Colleen McDannell and Bernhard Lang, *Heaven: A History*, 2nd ed. (New Haven: Yale University Press, 2001), 303–6.
7. Joan Hedrick, *Harriet Beecher Stowe: A Life* (New York: Oxford, 1994), 191.
8. J. C. Furnas, *The Americans: A Social History of the United States, 1587–1914* (New York: G. P. Putnam's Sons, 1969), 552.
9. Susan Bogert Warner [aka Elizabeth Wetherell], *The Wide, Wide World*, Chapter XLII, (Philadelphia: J. B. Lippincott, 1892), http://digital.library.upenn.edu/women/warner-susan/wide/wide.html.
10. Hedrick, 191–92.
11. Ibid., 192.
12. Samuel Eliot Morison, Henry Steele Commager, and William E. Leuchtenburg, *Growth of the American Republic*, vol. 1, 6th ed. (New York: Oxford, 1969), 635.
13. Science Resources on the Net, "Ulysses Simpson Grant," http://www.geocities.com/peterroberts.geo/Relig-Politics/USGrant.html#rlg.
14. The Civil War, "Robert E. Lee's Religion," http://www.sonofthesouth.net/leefoundation/Lee_Religion.htm.
15. John Esten Cooke, *A Life of General Robert E. Lee* (New York: D. Appleton and Company, 1871), chapter 8, part 6.
16. Jeffrey Warren Scott and Mary Ann Jeffreys, "Fighters of Faith," *Christianity Today*, http://www.christianitytoday.com/holidays/memorial/features/33h034.html.
17. Ibid.
18. Ibid.
19. Chaplain Alan Farley, interview with the author, January 11, 2008.
20. Ken Burns, interview with the author, November 8, 2007.
21. Gardiner H. Shattuck Jr., "Revival in the Camp," *Christianity Today*, http://www.christianitytoday.com/holidays/memorial/features/33h028.html.

22. Ibid.
23. Ibid.
24. Ibid.
25. Ibid.
26. "A Refuge from the Storm," Evangelical Tract Society, Petersburg, VA, http://docsouth.unc.edu/imls/refuge/refuge.html.
27. Shotgun's Home of the American Civil War, "Civil War Letter From an Unknown Mother," http://www.civilwarhome.com/mothersltr.htm.

Chapter Nine: The Critical Period
1. Mabel B. Casner and Ralph H. Gabriel, *The Story of American Democracy*, 3rd ed. (New York: Harcourt, Brace & World, 1958), 380.
2. Henry Champion Deming, *Eulogy of Abraham Lincoln* (Hartford, CT: A. N. Clark & Co., 1865), 52.
3. *New York Times*, April 20, 1865.
4. N. L. Rice, D.D., *Sermon on the Death of Abraham Lincoln, Late President of the United States, Preached on the Occasion of the National Funeral* (New York: Wm. C. Bryant & Co., Printers, 1865).
5. David B. Chesebrough, *Phillips Brooks: Pulpit Eloquence* (Westport, CT: Greenwood Press, 2001), 125.
6. Ibid., 137.
7. Samuel Eliot Morison, Henry Steele Commager, and William E. Leuchtenburg, *Growth of the American Republic*, vol. 1, 6th ed. (New York: Oxford, 1969), 794–95.
8. Martin E. Marty, *Righteous Empire: The Protestant Experience in America* (New York: Harper & Row, 1970), 147.
9. Ibid.
10. Ibid., 144.
11. Ibid., 148.
12. Ibid., 146.
13. Sydney E. Ahlstrom, *A Religious History of the American People*, vol. 1 (Garden City, NY: Image Books, 1975), 738.
14. Ibid., 736.
15. William R. Moody, *The Life of Dwight L. Moody* (New York: Fleming H. Revell, 1900), 430.
16. Ibid., 430–31.
17. Ibid., 431.
18. Stanley N. Gundry, *Love Them In: The Life and Theology of D. L. Moody* (Chicago: Moody, 1976), 97.
19. Ibid., 98.
20. Ibid.
21. D. L. Moody, "Hell" undated sermon, www.biblebelievers.com/moody_sermons/m7.html.
22. Thomas C. Oden, *Phoebe Palmer: Selected Writings* (New York: Paulist Press, 1998), 89.

23. Rebecca Price Janney, *Great Stories in American History* (Camp Hill, PA: Horizon Books, 1998), 107–8.

24. Charles Hodge, *Systematic Theology*, vol. 1 (London and New York: Thomas Nelson and Sons, 1871), 101, 364.

25. Edward McKinley, e-mail interview with author, November 30, 2007.

26. Ibid.

27. Ahlstrom, 745.

28. McKinley interview.

29. Ibid.

Chapter Ten: A Future, but What Kind of Hope?

1. Mark Twain, *Captain Stormfield's Visit to Heaven* (New York: Harper & Brothers, 1909), http://emotionalliteracyeducation.com/classic_books_online/cptsf10.htm.

2. PBS NewsHour Extra, "Mark Twain," June 27, 2001, http://www.pbs.org/newshour/extra/features/jan-june01/twain.html.

3. Ibid.

4. James Kirby Martin and others, *A Concise History of America and Its People* (New York: HarperCollins College Publishers, 1995), 449–50.

5. Dr. Robert Weiner, e-mail interview with the author, February 18, 2008.

6. Ting Ting Yan Davis, e-mail interview with the author, February 13, 2008.

7. Robert A. Divine and others, *America, Past and Present*, 4th ed. (New York: HarperCollins College Publishers, 1995), 672.

8. Ibid., 673.

9. George M. Marsden, *Fundamentalism and American Culture: The Shaping of Twentieth-Century Evangelicalism, 1870–1925* (New York: Oxford, 1980), 49.

10. Ibid., 51.

11. James H. Moorehead, *World Without End: Mainstream American Protestant Visions of the Last Things, 1880–1925* (Bloomington and Indianapolis: Indiana University Press, 1999), 1.

12. Billy Sunday Online, "The Life and Ministry of William Ashley Sunday," http://www.billysunday.org.

13. Marsden, 130.

14. Sydney E. Ahlstrom, *A Religious History of the American People*, vol. 1 (Garden City, NY: Image Books, 1975), 782

15. William James, *The Principles of Psychology*, vol. 1 (New York: Dover Publications, 1950), 127.

16. Ahlstrom, 775.

17. Ibid.

18. Ibid.

19. Walter Rauschenbusch, *A Theology of the Social Gospel* (New York: Abingdon Press, 1917), 108.

20. Ibid., 233–34.

21. Ibid.

22. Joseph Loconte, "Christianity Without Salvation: The Legacy of the 'Social Gospel'—100 Years Later," *Wall Street Journal*, May 11, 2007, http://opinionjournal.com/

taste/?id=110010062.

23. Russell T. Conwell, "The History of Fifty-Seven Cents," retyped from the publication of the sermon in *The Temple Review*, the weekly magazine of the Baptist Temple, v. 21, no. 7, December 19, 1912, Conwellana-Templana Collection/University Archives, Temple University Libraries, August 1997.

24. Martin E. Marty, *Righteous Empire: The Protestant Experience in America* (New York: Harper & Row, 1970), 150.

25. Ibid., 208.

Chapter Eleven: Cracks in the Dike

1. Charles S. Olcott, *The Life of William McKinley*, vol. 1 (Boston: Houghton Mifflin, 1916), 19.

2. Sydney E. Ahlstrom, *A Religious History of the American People*, vol. 1 (Garden City, NY: Image Books, 1975), 879.

3. Ibid.

4. Ibid., 879–80.

5. "William McKinley," The History Channel Web site, http://www.history.com/presidents/mckinley.

6. The Buffalo History Works, "The Funeral of William McKinley," http://www.buffalohistoryworks.com/panamex/assassination/funeral.htm.

7. The Cyber Hymnal, "Nearer, My God, To Thee," Adams and Bickersteth, http://www.cyberhymnal.org/htm/n/m/nmgtthee.htm.

8. Everett Marshall, *Complete Life of William McKinley and Story of His Assassination*, (n.p.: 1901), 395–96, http://mckinleydeath.com/documents/books/CLWMch39.htm.

9. Humanities Web, "Eulogy in Memory of William McKinley," http://www.humanitiesweb.org/human.php?s=r&p=a&a=i&ID=1668.

10. H. W. Brands, *TR: The Last Romantic* (New York: Basic Books, 1997), 411–12.

11. Enotes.com, "Medicine and Health at the Beginning of the Century," http://www.enotes.com/1900-medicine-health-american-decades.

12. Paul Strand, "The Lasting Impact of the Azusa Street Revival," CBN News, http://www.cbn.com/cbnnews/usnews/060424a.aspx.

13. Patricia Yollin, *San Francisco Chronicle*, "The Great Quake: 1906–2006: The Personal Hand," Sunday, April 9, 2006, http://www.sfgate.com/cgi-bin/article.cgi?f=/c/a/2006/04/09/BAGQ09DIARIES.DTL.

14. Carle Nolte, "The Great Quake," *San Francisco Chronicle*, Tuesday, April 11, 2006.

15. "The San Francisco Earthquake, 1906," EyeWitness to History Web site, http://www.eyewitnesstohistory.com/sfeq.htm.

16. Nolte.

17. "The San Francisco Earthquake, 1906," EyeWitness to History Web site.

18. D. A. Carson, *The Gagging of God* (Grand Rapids, MI: Zondervan Publishing House, 1996), 21.

19. Rev. Dr. James Galyon, comment on "Not even God could sink her!" 2 Worlds Collide Blog, comment posted on April 14, 2007, http://drjamesgalyon.wordpress.com/2007/04/14/"not-even-god-could-sink-her"/.

20. Ibid.

21. Ahlstrom, 881.
22. Ibid., 882.
23. Ibid., 884.
24. Ibid., 883.
25. Ibid.
26. Ibid., 885.
27. Pat Robertson, *The New World Order* (Waco, TX: Word, 1991), 51.

Chapter Twelve: A Lost Generation
1. John A. Garraty and Robert A. McCaughey, *The American Nation: A History of the United States*, 6th ed. (New York: Harper & Row, 1987), 730.
2. Alice K. Turner, *The History of Hell* (Orlando: Harcourt Brace & Company, 1993), 240–41.
3. A. G. Stock, *W. B. Yeats: His Poetry and Thought* (Cambridge: Cambridge, 1961), 109, 186.
4. Sydney E. Ahlstrom, *A Religious History of the American People*, vol. 1 (Garden City, NY: Image Books, 1975), 719.
5. T. S. Eliot, *T. S. Eliot: Selected Poems* (New York: Harcourt, Brace & World, 1964), 77–80.
6. George M. Marsden, *Fundamentalism and American Culture: The Shaping of Twentieth-Century Evangelicalism, 1870–1925* (New York: Oxford, 1980), 3.
7. Ibid., 3–4.
8. J. Gresham Machen, *Christianity and Liberalism* (Grand Rapids: Wm. B. Eerdmans, 1923), 7.
9. On the Internet at http://www.biola.edu/about/doctrinal-statement/.
10. On the Internet at http://www.pbu.edu/info/doctrine.htm.
11. Mark Galli and Ted Olsen, *131 Christians Everyone Should Know* (Nashville: Broadman & Holman, 2000), 104.
12. Church Education Resource Ministries, "Liberal Christianity," http://www.cerm.info/bible_studies/Topical/liberal_christianity.htm.
13. Harry Emerson Fosdick, *Christianity and Progress* (New York: Fleming H. Revell, 1922), 173.
14. Garraty and McCaughey, 724.
15. Doug Linder, "H. L. Mencken, 1880–1956," http://www.law.umkc.edu/faculty/projects/ftrials/scopes/menckenh.htm.
16. Ibid.
17. Edward J. Larson, *Summer for the Gods: The Scopes Trial and America's Continuing Debate over Science and Religion* (Cambridge: Harvard, 1997), 205.
18. Doug Linder, "William Jennings Bryan, 1860–1925," http://www.law.umkc.edu/faculty/projects/ftrials/scopes/bryanw.htm.
19. Larson, 203.
20. Ibid., 205.
21. Ibid.
22. Paxton Hibben, *The Peerless Leader, William Jennings Bryan* (New York: Farrar and Rinehart, 1929), 388.

23. Rebecca Price Janney, *Great Stories in American History* (Camp Hill, PA: Horizon Books, 1998), 127.

Chapter Thirteen: Depression and the Good War

1. John A. Garraty and Robert A. McCaughey, *The American Nation: A History of the United States*, 6th ed. (New York: Harper & Row, 1987), 658.
2. Sydney E. Ahlstrom, *A Religious History of the American People*, vol. 1 (Garden City, NY: Image Books, 1975), 924.
3. Martin E. Marty, *Righteous Empire: The Protestant Experience in America* (New York: Harper & Row, 1970), 236.
4. Ibid.
5. Ibid., 237.
6. H. Richard Niebuhr, Wilhelm Pauck, and Francis P. Miller, *The Church Against the World* (Chicago: Willett, Clark and Company, 1935), http://www.religion-online.org/showbook.asp?title=412.
7. Charles C. Brown, *Niebuhr and His Age: Reinhold Niebuhr's Prophetic Role and Legacy* (New York: Continuum International Publishing Group, 2002), 88.
8. Christopher W. Morgan and Robert A. Peterson, *Hell Under Fire: Modern Scholarship Reinvents Eternal Punishment* (Grand Rapids: Zondervan, 2004), 26.
9. Joel A. Carpenter, *Revive Us Again: The Reawakening of American Fundamentalism* (New York: Oxford, 1997), xii.
10. Catherine Marshall, *A Man Called Peter* (Grand Rapids: Chosen Books, 1951), 241.
11. Ken Burns, interview with the author, November 8, 2007.
12. Tom Brokaw, *The Greatest Generation* (New York: Random House, 1998), 55.
13. Ibid.
14. Ibid., 56.
15. Ibid., 336.
16. Charles White, e-mail interview with the author, March 31, 2008.
17. Donald F. Crosby, *Battlefield Chaplains: Catholic Priests in World War II* (Lawrence, KS: University Press of Kansas, 1994), 57.
18. Ibid., 102.
19. Wilfred "Mac" McCarty, e-mail interview with the author, March 28, 2008.
20. Rebecca Price Janney, *Great Stories in American History* (Camp Hill, PA: Horizon Books, 1998), 136–39.
21. Ibid.
22. Ibid.
23. Ibid.
24. Ibid.
25. McCarty interview.

Chapter Fourteen: The Post-War Era: Anxiety and Assurance

1. Billy Graham, "Heaven or Hell," Charlotte, NC, October 15, 1958, http://www.wheaton.edu/bgc/archives/docs/bg-charlotte/1015.html.
2. "We Will Bury You!" *Time*, November 26, 1956, http://www.time.com/time/magazine/article/0,9171,867329,00.html.

3. Sydney E. Ahlstrom, *A Religious History of the American People*, vol. 1 (Garden City, NY: Image Books, 1975), 959.

4. Ibid., 954.

5. Wikipedia, "Fulton J. Sheen," http://en.wikipedia.org/wiki/Fulton_J._Sheen.

6. Catholic Citizens of Illinois, "The Sainthood of Fulton Sheen," http://catholiccitizens. org/press/contentview.asp?c=10494.

7. Thomas C. Reeves, *America's Bishop: The Life and Times of Fulton J. Sheen* (San Francisco: Encounter Books, 2001), 30.

8. Ibid., 334.

9. Joseph Loconte, "A Mind That Grasped Both Heaven and Hell," *The New York Times*, November 22, 2003, http://query.nytimes.com/gst/fullpage.html?res=9803E6DE123B F931A15752C1A9659C8B63&sec=&spon=&pagewanted=all.

10. Wayne Martindale and Walter Hooper, *Beyond the Shadowlands: C. S. Lewis on Heaven and Hell* (Wheaton, IL: Crossway Books, 2005), 38.

11. Dr. Donald Grey Barnhouse, "The Sovereignty of God," Shiloh Online Library, http:// www.shilohonline.org/articles/barnhouse/tsog.htm.

12. Tony Rose, comment on "Barnhouse on 'Vincent Peale,' a story from Walter Martin," GalatiansC4V16 blog, comment posted on January 15, 2007, http://galatiansc4v16. wordpress.com/2007/01/15/barnhouse-on-vincent-peale-a-story-from-walter-martin/.

13. Roy Eckardt, *The Surge of Piety in America: An Appraisal* (New York: Association Press, 1958), 94.

14. Ibid., 182.

15. John A. Garraty and Robert A. McCaughey, *The American Nation: A History of the United States*, 6th ed. (New York: Harper & Row, 1987), 869.

16. "The Heart Stops Beating," *Time*, Monday, March 16, 1953, http://www.time.com/time/ magazine/article/0,9171,935822-1,00.html.

17. Ibid.

18. Ibid.

19. "Dr. Albert Einstein Dies in Sleep at 76; World Mourns Loss of Great Scientist," *The New York Times*, April 19, 1955.

20. Alex Guinness, *Blessings in Disguise* (New York: Random House, 1985), 34–35.

21. David Halberstam, *The Fifties* (New York: Villard Books, 1993), 484.

22. Adherents.com, "The Religious Affiliation of Rock and Roll Star Buddy Holly," http:// www.adherents.com/people/ph/Buddy_Holly.html.

Chapter Fifteen: Eve of Destruction?

1. Inaugural Address of President John F. Kennedy, January 21, 1961, Washington, D.C., John F. Kennedy Presidential Library and Museum, http://www.jfklibrary.org/ Historical+Resources/Archives/Reference+Desk/SpeechesJFK/003POF03Inaugural01 201961.htm.

2. Charles R. Morris, *A Time of Passion: America from 1960–1980* (New York: Harper & Row, 1984), 7.

3. Funeral sermon by Martin Luther King Jr., September 18, 1963, The Martin Luther King Jr., Research and Education Institute, http://www.stanford.edu/group/King/

publications/speeches/Eulogy_for_the_martyred_children.html.

4. Ibid.

5. Sydney E. Ahlstrom, *A Religious History of the American People*, vol. 1 (Garden City, NY: Image Books, 1975), 1079, 1083.

6. Eulogy at the Capitol Rotunda, November 24, 1963, John F. Kennedy Presidential Library and Museum, http://www.jfklibrary.org/Historical+Resources/Archives/Reference+Desk/Eulogies+to+the+Late+President+Kennedy.htm.

7. Ibid.

8. Ibid.

9. Marilyn Monroe and the camera Web site, "Marilyn Facts," http://www.marilynmonroe.ca/camera/about/facts/funeral.html.

10. Wikiquote, "John Lennon," http://en.wikiquote.org/wiki/John_Lennon.

11. All quotes from Charles V. McHugh are taken from an interview with the author, April 12, 2008.

12. "I've Been to the Mountaintop," speech by Martin Luther King Jr., April 3, 1968, AFSCME, http://www.afscme.org/about/1549.cfm.

13. Robert F. Kennedy quoting Aeschylus, April 4, 1968.

14. Benjamin Mays, "Benjamin Mays delivers King eulogy," April 9, 1968, Bates College, http://www.bates.edu/x49908.xml.

15. "A Life on the Way to Death," *Time*, June 14, 1968, http://www.time.com/time/magazine/article/0,9171,900110,00.html.

16. Ibid.

17. Senator Edward M. Kennedy at St. Patrick's Cathedral, June 8, 1968, John F. Kennedy Presidential Library and Museum, http://www.jfklibrary.org/Historical+Resources/Archives/Reference+Desk/Speeches/EMK/Tribute+to+Senator+Robert+F.+Kennedy.htm.

18. John Karraker, e-mail interview with the author, April 15, 2008.

19. Steve Daly, "A Hit of Biblical Proportions," *Entertainment Weekly* Web site, http://www.ew.com/ew/article/0,,293347,00.html.

20. Norman Greenbaum, e-mail interview with the author, October 13, 2006.

21. Rebecca Price Janney, *Great Stories in American History* (Camp Hill, PA: Horizon Books, 1998), 171–75.

22. Ahlstrom, 1094.

23. Ibid., 1086.

Chapter Sixteen: Anything Goes

1. "Lyndon Johnson, 1908–1973," *Time*, February 4, 1983, http://www.time.com/time/magazine/article/0,9171,906808,00.html.

2. Charles Colson, *Against the Night* (Ann Arbor, MI: Servant Publications, 1989), 43.

3. *Star Wars Episode IV: A New Hope.*

4. Benton Johnson, Dean R. Hoge, and Donald A. Luidens, "Mainline Churches: The Real Reason for Decline," *First Things*, March 1993, http://www.firstthings.com/article.php3?id_article=5100.

5. Ibid.

6. Bob and Gretchen Passantino, "What Do They Believe?" *Moody*, April 1992, 16.

7. Quoted by Martin Marty in his 1984 Ingersoll Lecture at Harvard University, "Hell Disappeared—No One Noticed. A Civic Argument."

8. *New Pittsburgh Courier*, January 13, 1973, reprinted in "Roberto Clemente: The Great One," The American Experience, PBS, http://www.pbs.org/wgbh/amex/clemente/press/news_1972b.html.

9. NASA History Division, "Challenger STS 51-L Accident," http://history.nasa.gov/sts51l.html.

10. All Challenger quotes, ibid.

Chapter Seventeen: From Here to Eternity

1. Arlington National Cemetery Web site, "Jacqueline Bouvier Kennedy Onassis," http://www.arlingtoncemetery.net/jbk.htm.

2. Lance Morrow, "The Stylishness of Her Privacy," *Time*, May 30, 1994, http://www.time.com/time/magazine/article/0,9171,980818-2,00.html.

3. Lynne Duke, "Family Memorializes Another JFK," *Washington Post*, Saturday, July 24, 1999, A1, http://www.washingtonpost.com/wp-srv/national/longterm/jfkjr/stories/kennedy072499.htm.

4. Kevin Merida, "Death of a Celebrity: An American Ritual," *Washington Post*, Thursday, July 22, 1999, C1, http://www.washingtonpost.com/wp-srv/national/longterm/jfkjr/stories/ritual072299.htm#TOP.

5. Ibid.

6. Ellen Goodman, "Shopping for a religion, like everything else," Tuesday, March 4, 2008, *The Intelligencer*, Doylestown, PA, A12.

7. Bill Keane, "The Family Circus," October 5, 2003, United Features Syndicate.

8. Pat Robertson, telephone interview with the author, November 15, 2007.

9. Randy Alcorn, "The Great Beyond," *Today's Christian Woman*, January/February 2008, 37.

10. Ibid., 38.

11. Philip G. Ryken, e-mail interview with the author, April 22, 2008.

12. Christopher C. Sutton, e-mail interview with the author, April 23, 2008.

13. Robertson interview.

14. *The Oprah Winfrey Show*, April 24, 2007.

15. "Come, Now Is the Time to Worship," Brian Doersken, 1998.

16. George Arthur Buttrick, ed., *The Interpreter's Bible*, vol. 11 (Nashville: Abingdon, 1955), 51.

17. Richard Ostling, "Heaven and Hell: 77% See Themselves in Heaven, Poll Finds; Scholars Sense Eroding of Traditional Belief," Religion, *Decatur Daily*, June 17, 2006, http://legacy.decaturdaily.com/decaturdaily/religion/060617/heaven.shtml.

18. Bill Newcott, "Life After Death," *AARP*, September/October 2007, 70.

19. Ibid.

20. Ibid.

21. Patrick Beach, "After-Life Experience: Still Writing: Texas Author Shrake 'Just Never Stops,'" Cox News Service, Sunday, February 3, 2008, Greater Philadelphia Newspapers, 5.

22. Erin Curry, "Study: Most Protestants believe Jesus is only way to salvation," Baptist Press News, October 14, 2004, http://www.bpnews.net/printerfriendly.asp?ID=19349.

23. Clark Pinnock, *A Wideness in God's Mercy* (Grand Rapids: Zondervan, 1992), 171.

24. Wolfgang Beinert and Francis Schussler Fiorenza, eds., *Handbook of Catholic Theology* (New York: Crossroad, 1995), 325.

25. Pope John Paul II, "Heaven, Hell and Purgatory," EWTN Libraries, http://www.ewtn .com/library/PAPALDOC/JP2HEAVN.htm.

Epilogue

1. C. S. Lewis, *Mere Christianity* (New York: Macmillan, 1952), 118.

2. Randy Alcorn, *Heaven* (Wheaton, IL: Tyndale, 2004), 444.

3. Joni Earickson Tada, *When God Weeps* (Grand Rapids: Zondervan, 1997), 196–97.

4. Joe Drenth, e-mail interview with the author, May 5, 2008.

5. Ibid.

6. Ibid.

7. Nancy Gibbs and Michael Duffy, "Billy Graham on Life Without Ruth," *Time*, August 8, 2007, http://www.time.com/time/nation/article/0,8599,1651115,00.html?iid=sphere-inline-sidebar.

8. Tada, 186, 192.

9. Ibid.

10. Pat Robertson, telephone interview with the author, November 15, 2007.

11. Charles Colson, *Against the Night* (Ann Arbor, MI: Servant Publications, 1989), 65, 69.

12. Robertson interview.

13. Beverly Roberts Gaventa, *First and Second Thessalonians* (Louisville: Westminster John Knox, 1998), 67.

ACKNOWLEDGMENTS

So many people have blessed me beyond measure during this project, from inception to conclusion. The prayers of my One Heart Sisters, MOPs, and Homebuilders Adult Bible Fellowship of First Baptist Church, Doylestown, and so many friends and family members sustained and encouraged me. To those who offered both their prayers and scholarly expertise, I thank my pastor, Chris Sutton, and my brothers in Christ Gary Shogren, Stan Key, Dan Young, and John Karraker. I am also indebted to Edward McKinley of Asbury College for his ever-present help, as well as Philip Ryken of Tenth Presbyterian Church, Philadelphia, Peter Lillback of the Providence Forum, Pat Robertson, and Martin Marty for their sensitive and scholarly insights. For helping me better understand the people of other eras and cultures I wish to thank Ting Ting Yan Davis, Robert Weiner, and Ken Burns. To those who shared their personal experiences with me, I am especially appreciative, including Joe Drenth, Wilfred McCarty, Charles White, and Charles McHugh.

Tamela Hancock Murray is my energetic agent whose belief in this project has helped make it possible. I am also endlessly thankful for friends who have helped in so many ways, especially Vera Cendrowski, who was my first reader while juggling life with three girls, Marlo Schalesky for her constant support while juggling life with four girls, Tricia Goyer for sharing her World War II buddies with me, and Sylvia Eagono, who has believed in me throughout our long and beautiful friendship. Thanks, also, to my vibrant exercise pals at Twining Valley.

I could never have done this, or any of my other books, without the love and blessing of my precious husband, Scott, and my darling preschooler, David, who exhibited real patience while Mama wrote her book.

Finally, to You, Lord Jesus, for the awesome life You've made possible for me now, and for the bright promises of tomorrow. You are the Rock on which I stand.